Creative
Followership

In the Shadow of Greatness

Creative
Followership

In the Shadow of Greatness

My Journey to President of **Chick-fil-A**®
Jimmy Collins with Michael Cooley

Foreword by Truett Cathy

**Creative
Followership**™

Published by Looking Glass Books, Inc.
Decatur, Georgia

Quantity sales at discounts are available to nonprofit organizations, schools, and associations. Contact Creative Followership, LLC, www.creativefollowership.com

Creative Followership is a trademark of Creative Followership, LLC.

Chick-fil-A, a registered trademark of CFA Properties, Inc., is used with permission.

Printed in the United States of America.

Cover design: Irene Morris Design
Book design and composition: Burtch Hunter Design

All scripture quotations are taken from the New American Standard Bible (Lockman Foundation 1995). Used by permission.

Cover photo: © LdF / E+ / GettyImages

Library of Congress Cataloging-in-Publication Data

Collins, James L. S., 1936–
Creative Followership: In the Shadow of Greatness / by James L.S. Collins with Michael R. Cooley.

162 pp. 13.97 cm x 21.59 cm

ISBN 978-1-929619-48-1

1. Leadership. 2. Organizational behavior. 3. Cathy, S. Truett, 1921– 4. Chick-Fil-A Corporation. I. Title.

HD57.7.C6453 2013
650.1'3--dc23
2013010285

First Edition

I dedicate this work to my wife, Oleta,
and our children, Kenneth, Kathleen, and Susan.

J. C.

All of the stories in this book are from my real-life experiences. They are all true. Where appropriate, names have been changed to protect individual privacy. All of my references to anything that occurred while I was an employee of Chick-fil-A, Inc., are based on my memory of the events. My memory may vary from that of others. Statements about or involving Chick-fil-A policies, business practices, and legal issues are not intended to comply with correct legal terminology or current or past business policy or practices. Chick-fil-A, Inc., has not approved this book or authorized me to speak on its behalf.

He who tends the fig tree will eat its fruit,
And he who cares for his master will be honored.

KING SOLOMON (PROVERBS 27:18)

ACKNOWLEDGMENTS

I like books. Over the years people have urged me to write a book. I made notes, collected material and cataloged it, with the confidence that I would write a book, someday. It seemed like such a good idea, I even decided that I would write several books. Yet, time was passing and I still had not written a book.

I wanted to write because I had a lot to share, and still do. But, there were two barriers to my writing: I don't like to write and I don't write very well. My son-in-law, Michael Cooley, came to my rescue. Without him this book would not have been written. He took my outline; interviewed me and searched my files, recordings, and videos of more than 40 years; then wrote down what I wanted to say.

It sounds so simple, but believe me it was not easy or quickly accomplished.

In undertaking a project like this, I needed people who would tell me the truth, not what they thought I might want to hear. I thank all of those who proofread and did not hesitate to recommend improvements.

First of all, my wife, Oleta's, support and encouragement was the most important of all. She knows me better than anyone and has been my chief encourager for almost sixty years. When she said it was good, I knew I could proceed.

Mary Graybar helped me by raising my awareness of what I needed to do to appeal to the target audience. Her advice on story development was refreshing and enlightening. Charles Q. Carter's organizational and structural recommendations came just when I needed them. His time and wisdom arrived at a critical point in the development of the book.

Of special help was Steve Piersanti, who told me that the manuscript read like three different books. That encouraged me to prepare to use the material in three different books and also created a tremendous improvement in this book. Mark Miller freely shared his experience with me. I found great value in talking with someone who has "been there and done that."

Todd Manza's editing was very important. More than just correcting the grammar, misspellings, and typos, he offered many excellent suggestions. He did more than anyone else to make me comfortable with the finished product. His expertise gave me reassurance that the readers would view this book as a high-quality piece of work. With his help my confidence soared!

I looked for appealing book covers that caught my eye and made note of the designer of those covers. When I found that the same person designed five of my favorites, I was certain that Irene Morris was the designer we needed for a fresh and attention-grabbing cover. She understood both what we were trying to communicate and our target audience. I believe she hit the bull's-eye!

The main body of a book is its words. Those words convey nothing until they are read. When they are easy to read and flow comfortably from one thought to the next it makes reading a pleasure. That means that the design and composition is critical to the reader. I thank Burtch Hunter for taking the input from all of the interested parties, satisfying us all and creating a beautiful easy to read text!

There was one individual I found myself relying on again and again. Dick Parker, owner of Looking Glass Books, always seemed to have one more rabbit to draw out of his hat, at exactly the right moment. The sum of his expertise and knowledge was topped only by the generosity he offered of both his time and patience. With his considerable help and guidance, we finally have this book!

From a crude outline; through files, tapes, videos, and recollections; to a rough manuscript; through revisions uncounted and several rewrites—these are the people responsible for turning my thoughts into the book you are now reading. I like the book and hope you will too.

—Jimmy Collins

Contents

FOREWORD xv

PREFACE...xvii

INTRODUCTION xxiii

PART ONE: THE PHILOSOPHY *of* FOLLOWERSHIP

CHAPTER 1 Looking for Answers 1

CHAPTER 2 The Idea of Creative Followership 15

CHAPTER 3 The Shadow 22

CHAPTER 4 Fire Your Boss?...26

CHAPTER 5 Finding a New Boss.......................................38

PART TWO: THE PRINCIPLES *of* FOLLOWERSHIP

CHAPTER 6 The Journey Begins 50

CHAPTER 7 Mustangs and Mules......................................68

CHAPTER 8 Effectively Using Input and Feedback 85

CHAPTER 9 Taking Responsibility....................................111

CHAPTER 10 Exceeding Expectations...............................124

CHAPTER 11 Develop Yourself 135

CONCLUSION 161

⬆ Creative
Followership™

M ost of us have a desire to accomplish something bigger than we can accomplish alone. When we followers are drawn to a leader with an attractive vision, a unifying purpose, there is no limit to what we can accomplish together.

Followers choose to follow a leader with a compelling purpose, vision, cause, or goal, the unifying purpose. It is the leader's unifying purpose that attracts the interest and loyalty of followers. The leader is someone who is able to communicate the unifying purpose in a manner that is inspiring, persuasive, or motivating. The unifying purpose joins the followers to the leader.

The Creative Followership logo illustrates the three essential components of leadership, followership, and unifying purpose. The large arrow represents the unifying purpose. The small arrows represent the leader and followers, held together by the unifying purpose. The leader is in the center of the unifying purpose, out front, leading the followers. The followers have joined the leader and are supporting him in fulfilling the unifying purpose.

Creative Followership Principles

1 Choose Your Boss 31

2 Know Your Boss...58

3 Do What Your Boss Does Not Like to Do..............59

4 Do What Your Boss Does Not Do Well.................62

5 Do Not Compete with Your Boss 64

6 Make Your Boss Look Good................................66

7 Take Responsibility...68

8 Everyone Likes Problems 69

9 Do Not Hoard Authority.....................................70

10 It Is Better to Restrain Mustangs than Kick Mules 73

11 Do It the Way the Boss Likes It Done.................76

12 Let Others See the Boss in You...........................78

13 Help Your Boss Succeed.....................................80

14 Build Support in Advance...................................82

15 Gather, Interpret, Translate, Repackage...............86

16 The Only Real Feedback Is Negative 96

17 Cultivate Feedback..98

18 Ask for Suggestions Rather than Criticism 100

19 Always Apologize, Never Explain.........................102

20 Confront Grumbling and Murmuring 104

21 Encourage Your Boss..108

22 Make Your Decisions Good 115

23 Be Assertive 120

24 Learn to Say No 122

25 Do It Right...124

26 Do More than Is Expected 125

27 Do Not Wait to Be Told What to Do....................126

28 Do the Dirty and Difficult Jobs............................131

29 Take Risks..132

30 Bad News Does Not Improve with Age 134

31 Do Not Be Easily Discouraged.............................136

32 Be Thankful for Strong-Willed Critics 142

33 Never Assume What You Can Verify 145

34 Use Actions and Symbols....................................149

35 Avoid Executive Privilege....................................153

Truett Cathy and Jimmy Collins, 1993

FOREWORD

To excel in leadership you must first master follower-ship. Any person aspiring to be an effective executive would do well to read Jimmy Collins's book *Creative Followership: In the Shadow of Greatness*.

Jimmy Collins served effectively as president of Chick-fil-A and retired after 32 years of service. He demonstrated the role of followership. Jimmy respected my position as CEO and gave me his unwavering support. In making decisions, we were comfortable discussing issues and made it a point to agree on a solution. Jimmy's insight and vision helped prepare the young men and women of Chick-fil-A to be successful. Upon meeting Jimmy they immediately perceived his commitment, loyalty, and dedication to me and the vision I had for Chick-fil-A. He took my vision for Chick-fil-A and demonstrated exceptionally well how it could be implemented. These young people knew his intent and trusted Jimmy would direct them correctly in following my lead.

Chick-fil-A has become an industry leader due to the strong foundational principles practiced in the early years. We hear of businesses succeeding or failing, but it is not the business . . . it is the people who succeed or fail.

—S. Truett Cathy
Founder and CEO,
Chick-fil-A, Inc.

The year was 1979 and Chick-fil-A was only dreaming about the office facilities it would create and occupy in the next few years. At that point in my life, I had never tasted Chick-fil-A and I knew nothing about the company other than the logo and the jingle from their radio commercials. Roger Christian, the music director at my church, invited me to accompany him to Chick-fil-A's corporate headquarters for a meeting one afternoon. On the way there, he suggested I make it a point to look around and take note of the intense enthusiasm the office staff has for their brand. He said I would see the Chick-fil-A logo all around the office—on clock faces, men's ties, watches, coffee cups, banners, posters—it is nearly everywhere and is printed on everything.

What I experienced was not what I expected. The facility was not a high-rise midtown skyscraper but a not-so-very-impressive building surrounded by the noise of the Atlanta airport, a Ford Motor Company plant, and the rumbling of three active railroad tracks. But yes, the logo was everywhere! There was something unique about the place and the people I met that day. I was transformed by the aura of entrepreneurial energy—like nothing I had encountered up to that point in my nearly 18 years of life.

That is when I not only learned about Chick-fil-A but also met Dan T. Cathy, the exuberant son of founder S. Truett Cathy. Later, I would meet S. Truett Cathy when he came to speak at my church. Although the founder is usually the focal point of attention and credit, at some point most people will learn that great leaders achieve greatness because they intentionally surround themselves with people who support, advise, and successfully execute plans. Jimmy Collins was Truett's third full-time non-restaurant employee at the company headquarters. Jimmy was the one who supported, advised, and successfully executed the plans for Truett. When I met Jimmy, I assumed he was an accountant because he had such a large adding machine, and nothing about his demeanor said executive vice president—his title prior to being named president.

Jimmy was always reluctant to reveal his title. If asked what he did for a living, he would say, "I work for Chick-fil-A." If pressed for more details, he would answer, "I work at the home office." He has a one-of-a-kind approach and backs it up with decades of accumulated wisdom.

Another two years would pass before I visited the corporate office again. This time the office was in a brand-new facility and I was not there to look for logos. Jimmy and I met behind the seldom-closed doors of his office. It was the day I told him I wanted to marry his daughter Susan. More than just a father-in-law, Jimmy Collins became a lifelong mentor.

I, like many others, have learned many things from Jimmy. If this book is titled *In the Shadow of Greatness,* I suppose you could say I am a witness to one in the shadow of greatness. It did not seem to matter what the issue was—whether it was about work or business or ministry—this is the guy countless people turned to, almost covertly at times, seeking advice about decision making and dealing with difficult people or situations.

So, what is so special about this man? Does he possess secret knowledge? Is there a formula that he follows? Would he please share it? How can one guy know so much about the right things to say in so many diverse circumstances? How does he manage to be both confrontational and complimentary at the same time?

Over the years I tried to steal hints and clues. Sometimes I would bring up questions during family dinners or on vacations at the beach. I would ask, "What would you think/do/say if . . ." and then he would tell me what he would do in a scenario similar to the one I made up. The answers usually came quickly and cut right to the heart of the issue.

The learning went much faster when I saw Jimmy in action, in person with Chick-fil-A Operators. In 1999, I was working in the executive office of the North American Mission Board of the Southern Baptist Convention. Dan Cathy invited me to see the annual Chick-fil-A Operators Seminar production process in action. The event was held at the Fontainebleau hotel in Miami, Florida. It was there that I had the opportunity to see Jimmy deep in his element, speaking at the annual event.

In 2004, three years after Jimmy retired, I found myself back at the Operators Seminar, working for Jimmy's successor, the new president of the company, Dan Cathy. Over the next six years, I served as an independent contractor working on special projects for Dan. Jimmy had left the building, but his mark lingered on. I was fortunate to be involved in meetings with the upper-level executive decision makers. When decisions were most critical and the deliberations seemed stalled, someone would ask, "What would Jimmy do?"

I mistakenly believed I had caught on to most of his principles over the years, but I only had the tip of the iceberg. Working on this book, I realized I had failed to grasp the bigger picture. All I knew was that if I wanted to become a person who knew how to make career, business, and ministry choices, I would have to get inside his head and learn how he sees these things. There was no way to put everything together and understand the foundational principles until I sat down and examined the long butcher-paper lists I had taped on all four walls of my office. I gradually came to a clearer understanding of what followership is—something entirely different from anything out there on the business bookshelves.

Decades of Jimmy's personal notes had to be reviewed, years of audio and video recordings had to be played—plus the many days of one-on-one Q & A sessions we shared. The process took several years, and new insights opened up all the way to the moment the manuscript was completed.

What you are about to read is based on one man's personal experience. I am certain you will not read what is written here anywhere else. Clearly, this is not a repackaged collection of ideas from someone else. The bricks and mortar of this book are based on the principles that Jimmy Collins lived out in the real world of business and the day-to-day challenges of his career.

Jimmy helped build a preeminent restaurant business serving a cross section of the public. This required him to focus on customer satisfaction. Although his desk was in the corporate office, his job extended well beyond the tastefully decorated halls of the office building. I should also mention that he has never conducted any academic research projects like those upon which many business books are based. What he presents here is practical and will work at any level of responsibility. It is highly transferable, useable in almost any organization. These principles have properties that will bring predictable results in a variety of different circumstances.

As I was compiling the information in this book, I kept asking myself, "What if I had known these principles when I was 21? How differently would I have handled many situations if I had known then what I know now?"

When you finish reading this book, you will likely be looking at things much differently. Whether or not you agree with everything Jimmy says, you will gain a unique perspective on the notion of being a follower. Most of you will find yourselves thinking differently about leadership, success, and what it means to work with others.

—Michael Cooley

INTRODUCTION

During my years with Chick-fil-A, Inc., I had the pleasure of meeting with many people who wanted to discuss their career. As you would guess, some of those I met with were already part of Chick-fil-A, and even more were interested in exploring the possibility of a Chick-fil-A career, but a surprisingly large number were pursuing careers in other companies or organizations.

To have many people wanting advice to help them on their path to success did not seem strange to me. Early in my career, it was exactly what I had searched for but seldom found. Actually, my search never stopped, even though it was rare indeed for me to meet person-to-person with anyone to discuss my career. Almost all of my personal and professional development was fed by books, tapes, and seminars.

As I look back I see, with the twenty-twenty vision that comes as standard equipment with reminiscing, how valuable personal career counseling could have been. But access to the right advisers did not seem open to me early in my career, and I seriously doubt that you find it any easier than I did.

Don't despair. I can help you.

As a result of those many sessions I had with men and women wanting my advice, I have a clear idea of what you want to know, and it is not what you are likely to get anywhere else. How can I say this?

It is easy for me understand the questions and issues confronting people searching for the path to a successful career because I have been there. From an early age I dreamed of a successful career as a corporate executive. Along the way, through a process of trial and error, I discovered principles that helped me achieve the career I really wanted. I will offer you the same advice I have extended countless times in one-on-one meetings.

When I had discussions with someone wanting career advice, I let him or her do most of the talking. I listened. There is no point in helping a man get on a train until I know his destination. They all wanted to know the keys to creating a successful career, to getting along with their boss, and to getting along with their coworkers. However, the most frequent discussions centered around getting along with the boss. It was not the only area of discussion—in fact, we usually started with other discussion topics—but it took first priority by a wide margin, followed by coworker relationships.

Because it is most likely that you don't know me and probably know very little about me, you may wonder why most of those one-on-one meetings would be tilted in that direction. Here is why.

Many years ago I created a career approach that is different from anything I ever read about or heard anyone describe. I have named my career approach Creative Followership. Creative Followership is based on principles that are highly transferable; they will work for anyone in any organization.

Followership principles can get you where you want to go, no matter where you are in your life and career or what job title you now hold. Not only that, but as you begin to apply and live out these principles, you will begin to make and develop principles of your own. It is possible for you, through Creative Followership, to create the kind of career you have been dreaming about.

Creative Followership enabled me to create a rewarding relationship with my boss, S. Truett Cathy, the founder and CEO of Chick-fil-A. We had a relationship built on trust and mutual respect. Because our work was very public in nature and we did not work from behind closed doors, many people witnessed how we communicated and saw how decisions were being made. There was a lot of curiosity about how our relationship worked. I have always been happy to share my experiences with anyone who wanted to learn more.

After I retired from Chick-fil-A, I continued sharing Creative Followership. I left an open invitation for people to call me if they wanted to talk. I retired in 2001, and I still receive calls and requests for one-on-one meetings.

A wide variety of people make appointments to see me. They range from senior executives to entry-level associates. These meetings are opportunities for me to listen attentively and then share how to apply the appropriate principles of Creative Followership.

The response I receive when I speak with someone about followership for the first time is interesting, because what I tell them is so much different from what they were expecting to hear. People accustomed to the well-known leadership experts find the strategy of not trying to be the leader quite foreign to the way they have been conditioned to think.

In my experience and opinion, the common approach of popular leadership training and development experts does not teach people to be leaders. Yet the experts are constantly writing new books that quickly make it to the best-seller list because so many people want to learn how to enhance their careers. Too many leadership experts would have you believe that all you have to do to become a leader is to comply with their (insert any number) steps. Whether the number of steps is ten easy ones or one hundred hard ones, I don't believe just complying with them will make anyone a leader. If that were all it took to become a leader, would I be the only follower left? I have a problem with books that claim to teach people how to be leaders, because I am convinced that leadership cannot be taught.

When I am asked about my leadership philosophy, my reply is, "My focus has been on followership, not leadership." This book will not teach you to be a leader—I do not claim to be an expert on leadership. I will share with you what worked for me, and what worked for me was followership.

Sharing the principles of Creative Followership is always very gratifying. The supportive feedback I get in return is a motivator to continue. I enjoy spending time with people, not sitting before a keyboard and monitor.

However, the idea of recording these principles on paper began, over time, to grow on me. The encouragement I received from friends whose opinions I highly regard was, "Jimmy, you should write a book on followership." With the support of friends and former colleagues, and the assistance of Michael Cooley, I accepted the challenge. My effort will be another opportunity to share these principles and how to use them with one more person—you.

Discovering these principles was an exciting process; applying them made my career journey a satisfying and successful adventure. What worked for me was not focusing on leadership but practicing followership. I am confident what worked for me will work for you.

—Jimmy Collins

PART ONE

THE PHILOSOPHY
— *of* —
FOLLOWERSHIP

CHAPTER 1

Looking for Answers

One day a curious reporter asked Abraham Lincoln how long it took him—start to finish—to compose what would become the most famous presidential speech in U.S. history, the Gettysburg Address. After a moment of reflection, Lincoln answered matter-of-factly, "All of my life."

That was probably not the answer the reporter was expecting, but this reply conveys incredible depth and wisdom. What Lincoln was saying is that anyone who does a job—and does it well—can claim the job took a lifetime to complete. We bring the sum total of our life experiences to every task in life; we bring our mistakes and our successes. We take everything we have learned with us to future tasks.

If you were to ask how long it took me to write this book, I would tell you I have been in the process of writing it all of my life. In some form or another, all the things I have learned, everything I have experienced, and what I have observed are a part of this book. This book summarizes many experiences of my life journey.

Along the way, through trial and error, I discovered a different approach to success and satisfaction: Creative Followership. I believe that, by putting it to work in your life, you can make yourself more successful and enjoy a more satisfying career.

Have you ever thought, "I want to be successful" and "I want a better job, with more responsibility and authority," but wondered how you could make it happen? I had those same thoughts.

MY SEARCH FOR ANSWERS

I was confident at an early age that I knew who I wanted to be and where I wanted to go. I didn't know how to get there. I didn't have a clue. But I was sure there were answers, if I could just find them.

Initially, I marched off in search of definite and precise answers. Surely, someone knew the answers and they had been written down somewhere, maybe in a book with a good index, so it would be easy to find whatever I wanted to know. Before you laugh and say, "That's kid stuff," go look inside most of the leadership books on the shelf of your nearest bookstore. That approach did not work for me and I doubt that it will work for you.

Even though my life was cluttered with definite questions, precise answers were seldom solutions. I soon learned that every answer leads to more questions. Think of the child's response to every answer: "Why?" "Why?" Why?"

I also learned that a single answer is seldom the solution for the same question more than once. When the same question arises in two different situations, even for the same person, the circumstances are always different. Keep in mind that I am not referring to mathematical formulas.

Fortunately, even as I realized that my search for single and precise answers would never be fruitful, I also learned that I didn't need them. What I really needed were guiding principles that would help me navigate life's many troubled waters to reach the destination of my choice.

This is the story of how my search started and vignettes of my discovery of the principles of Creative Followership.

THE EARLY YEARS

My parents, Horace and Medley Collins, were hard-working farmers—sharecroppers, to be precise. My family raised cotton near the base of Kennesaw Mountain in Cobb County, Georgia. My father did not have his hands on the reins of a big corporation, looking out at a panoramic view of the city from a high-rise corner office. Instead, his hands gripped real leather reins, with a view of a field, from behind a mule pulling a plow. Working the fields of sunbaked Georgia soil

Horace and Medley Collins with their children, Ray, Roy, Tommy, Jimmy, and Ellen, 1942

was backbreaking work, risky, and not an easy way to make a living.

I learned firsthand what hard work was like; I learned on the farm. My first work-for-pay experience occurred at age 10, picking cotton, of course, for my uncle. I was full of confidence and anxious to make money fast. Cotton picking is not difficult to understand intellectually, and best of all it requires no prior experience. Cotton pickers do one thing: they fill up bags with cotton.

That morning I flew out the front door, confident that I was big and strong enough to take on the task. Expecting to finish the day with coins jingling in my pocket, I was raring to go. At the edge of the field, the boss, my uncle, gave me the instructions. I had two options: I could fill a big bag (the size the men used), and in return I would earn a quarter, or I could fill a small bag (the size the women used), and I would earn a dime. Since I wanted to make a lot of money fast, I asked for the big bag. My uncle talked me into using the small bag; it turned out to be for the best.

That day I learned how hard it was to earn a dime. In addition to the money, I earned bloody fingers—an unforeseen consequence of my labor. The day also taught me the realities of life awaiting anyone choosing a career as a cotton farmer.

As sundown approached, I was sitting there on the uneven, weathered planks of the front porch, looking out over the cotton field, contemplating my future. A fresh understanding of life interrupted my dream of getting rich by raising and picking cotton. With my tired feet dangling and swinging off the edge of the porch, I watched the last of the workers in their bib overalls or dungarees, long-sleeved shirts, and straw hats abandon the field for the day.

It occurred to me that all of my family wore heavy work clothes because they all earned their living doing the same thing: sharecropper farming. I knew I had to do whatever it took to go in a different direction. As the warm glow of the sun departed that evening, I formed a newly found determination to break away and do something else.

I knew for certain that bib overalls and dungarees were out of the question. When I went to work I was going to wear a white shirt, a tie, and a suit, dressed as a professional, an executive, a businessman. Now I just had to figure out how to make it happen. The journey was about to begin.

My prospect of success in business did not look promising. We all have times when the prospect of success seems unlikely. How could I, Jimmy Collins, son of a sharecropper, take that first step from the fields of hard Georgia clay to the polished floors of an office building? Where would I start? I needed someone to provide advice and guidance. I needed a role model.

LOOKING FOR ROLE MODELS

I could not meet with a successful executive for advice because I did not know one. The best I could do at the time was to start by watching the people in charge, no matter what their business. I was sure their behavior could be learned and copied. I was certain I not only could learn from them but also would someday outperform them. I just needed to pick out someone to copy.

Finding someone to copy was a huge challenge because I lacked any professional role models. What I did have at that time was a number of outstanding moral characters as role models. Learning and copying their examples shaped me and molded me from my earliest years.

One role model that stands out was my Aunt Ruth Bettis. Aunt Ruth gave me my first book, *Tom Swift and His Sky Racer*. I still have that book. At the time, the only book my family owned was the Bible. Aunt Ruth gave me more books, and she taught me that there is more to reading than just studying textbooks. I am thankful to her for those lessons. As an adult, my enthusiasm for reading is still alive and well. For a long time my goal has been to read 100 books each year. Being encouraged to read as child meant that, although professional role models were absent, I was able to learn by reading about them. My favorite building in East Point, the suburb of Atlanta where I grew up, is the public library. I spent many wonderful hours there.

Another monumental influence on my character and self-discipline was my maternal grandmother, Etna Waldrop. Grandma Waldrop came from the mountains of North Carolina. She told us grandchildren fascinating stories of her childhood. These stories not only were entertaining but also carried powerful moral lessons, wrapped up in her pictorial style of storytelling. When Grandma told a story, you were there in the midst of it, seeing, hearing, smelling, and feeling everything around you.

Grandma Waldrop read her Bible and prayed every day. Her favorite illustration of her disciplined life was that there were two things she had never done: attend a "moving picture show" or drink a Coca-Cola. (She was convinced Coke had cocaine in it.) Although I do occasionally

Grandma Etna Waldrop

go to movies and often drink Coca-Colas, I do follow her example of praying and reading my Bible every day. And although she was not a business executive mentor, I did learn valuable and practical moral life lessons from Grandma Waldrop. She was a perfect model of the power of personal discipline and determination.

Actually, I was surrounded by many good character models as a child, but I lacked executive models. Growing up, I did encounter a few local businessmen. I watched and learned as much as possible from their interactions and conversations. The point is that I did not let the lack of role models stop me from pursuing my goal. You might say I knew the what of my future but was still trying to find the how.

There are times when there does not seem to be a way to go, and suddenly life surprises us and changes course. Unexpectedly, doors open. My life changed forever with two words from my father: "We're moving." We were moving to Atlanta.

At that time, the country was in the midst of World War II. My father had attempted to join the army but could not pass the physical examination. However, industry was gearing up and creating jobs right here at home. My father got one of those new jobs. He moved from being a sharecropper in Cobb County to being a warehouseman in Atlanta. My family relocated.

It was a happy day; we were moving away from the farm. I was glad to get onto a different path. The good news is that it matters little where you come from or where you have been, because you have the freedom to choose who you will become and what you will do in the future. Perhaps you are thinking, just as I did out in that cotton field many years ago, "There has got to be a better way of making a living."

A ROLE MODEL AT LAST

When I was fifteen I joined the Civil Air Patrol Cadets, an auxiliary arm of the U.S. Air Force, organized to provide emergency services, aviation education, and a cadet program. The Civil Air Patrol made me feel important and was a way for a kid my age to get to wear a sharp-looking uniform. In addition, it offered me the opportunity to fly in all sorts of airplanes!

While I was in the Civil Air Patrol Cadets, I found my first model of a real leader, Shanton Granger. This guy really had it all together. Granger was our cadet commanding officer. He was coordinator of our training on downed airplane searches, and he was the one responsible for leading us to third place in the national drill team competition. Granger was well liked and respected by the adult leadership of the Civil Air Patrol.

Shanton Granger was a take-charge guy. No task ever seemed too difficult for him. Every problem was quickly and effortlessly solved, while at the same time he was able to keep everyone happy. He was everyone's friend but he was nobody's buddy. He mixed and mingled with everyone but was not a part of any specific clique. He could be funny, he was clever, he was serious, and he could be compassionate or stern, all in the right way at the right time. At that time, I concluded that Shanton Granger was whom I truly wanted to be like.

What a relief it was to finally find that role model! At some point, I imagine we all find at least one person we want to imitate. I know at the time I wanted to talk like, walk like, act like, and be like Granger. I was sure if I did I also would be a leader.

It was a great plan. At least it seemed like a great plan. Except for one little thing. It didn't work.

My first step in copying Granger was to look like him. The way he wore his hat caught my attention, this special way he cocked it at an angle over his right eyebrow. The first time I tried that with my hat, some of the guys made jokes about it. "Collins is trying to act like Granger." It was very embarrassing to be caught in the act of imitation. I didn't like being called a copycat.

From that day on, I determined I was going to be myself and make no apologies for it. I decided I would never copy anyone. I would be the original me.

When Tim Tassopoulos, the current executive vice president of operations, joined the Chick-fil-A staff as a consultant, he already had many years of experience as a part-time Chick-fil-A employee during high school, college, and graduate school. While visiting our Volusia Mall restaurant in Daytona Beach, Florida, franchise Operator Margaret Wilson Phillips asked him about his career goals within the organization. "What do you want to be, the next Jimmy Collins?" Tim's wise reply was, "No, the first Tim Tassopoulos."

Never try to become a copy of anyone else.
It never works.

The most important thing I learned from trying to copy Granger was that acting or behaving like a leader would not make me a leader. There was something about being a leader that I did not yet fully comprehend. I kept trying to figure out what I could do better, what steps I could put into practice to learn to become a leader. If I did those specific leadership things the right way, I would surely become a leader, right?

At that time, I was totally convinced that, to be satisfied and successful in life as an executive, I must be a leader. The desire was there; I wanted to be a leader. But something was still very wrong. I was missing something. I vowed to uncover the missing piece of the puzzle. I tried all I heard and all I was told I should do, but nothing seemed to work for me. I went from one setback to another.

However, these setbacks did not stop me from pursuing my dream. I knew that I had to keep pushing ahead if I wanted to reach my goals and make my dream a reality. I refused to become discouraged or think negative thoughts, even though I did not yet have a clue about how to become a businessman, the path was not clear, and I still had a lot to learn.

A DIFFERENT APPROACH

Where are you? Are you in a similar situation? Do you have what seems to be an unrealistic goal? I did. Do you feel that you may have been chasing the wrong rabbit? I did. Do you see others finding the answers that seem to fade away just as you reach for them? I did. But instead of discouraging or stopping me, my lack of success made me more determined. If imitating leaders would not make me a leader, there must be a way to learn leadership. I decided to look in another direction.

All of us at some time tend to search for and then settle

for answers that tickle our ears with promises they never can fulfill. I read the advertisements for books, tapes, and seminars that said, "Come to us and we will teach you to become a leader." I bought it. To say that I went for it hook, line, and sinker would be a gross understatement. I was willing to listen, I loved to read, and I found live presentations entertaining. This must be exactly what I had been looking for but was missing. The song in my heart was "Leadership, Here I Come."

My search for the answers to "How do I become a leader?" continued for seventeen years. In the process, I read scores of books, listened to hundreds of tapes, attended dozens of seminars, and followed many multistep processes. I did not become a leader.

What I got out of my search was a three-part lesson in reality. First, the experts on leadership don't even agree on a simple and common definition of leadership. So, the plain reality slowly became clear: if they can't define it, how can they teach it?

At this point you may want to ask, "Jimmy, did you waste your time and effort on that seventeen-year search?"

No! My search was very productive. I learned excellent management and general business techniques and very effective sales methods, and I gained insights into old tried-and-true business philosophies as well as the latest business and management experiments. I was able to sit at the feet of some of the masters of business and the greatest of all leaders. What I learned guided me through a constant and continuous personal development. I invented and then reinvented myself over and over again.

A wasted time? Oh, no! It was an enlightening journey, a time of expanding my personal and professional growth and development.

The second result of this search was that I finally realized leadership cannot be taught. Many fine, well-intentioned people can teach about leadership, but they cannot teach another person to become a leader.

Third, I learned the real definition of a leader: a person with followers.

So simple; so easy to understand. No wonder the journey of discovery was so long and hard.

At the same time that I discovered what a leader is, I also discovered what a follower is and what binds leaders and followers together.

It was as if someone had at last turned on the lights; now I could see that followership opened unlimited opportunities. For me, that discovery was like finding a treasure map that had been in my pocket all the time, leading to a treasure that had been right in front of me forever. Now I knew where to find success and satisfaction. With that map in hand, I set out on my followership journey, an adventure of a lifetime.

If you are prepared to think with your mind open and are ready for a different approach, I invite you to take this journey with me to Creative Followership.

CHAPTER 2

The Idea of Creative Followership

People ask me, "What changed the most during your career at Chick-fil-A?" The answer is simple: I did.

One of my favorite authors on executive development is Warren Bennis. He said that leaders "invent themselves." Think about it; it is true. And not only leaders; followers also invent themselves. We all have a choice. We can decide who we want to be and invent ourselves, or we can just drift through life and accept whatever we become. I decided to choose who I would be and to invent myself—and then I reinvented myself again and again.

I encourage you, in the beginning of your career, to invent yourself, and then never stop reinventing yourself. As you continue to grow and develop, the process will be exciting and satisfying. You will never be bored because each reinvention will be a new you.

No one can tell you how to reinvent yourself. This book will not attempt to do that; it is not a textbook or a self-help manual. It does not contain a list of how-to instructions. Instead, I will tell you what worked for me—it is up to you to decide what fits your situation.

Consider two things: where you are and where you would like to be. There should be a gap between those two answers; make sure you are honest with yourself as you answer both questions. Before you start your journey, you must know where you are starting and where you want to go.

Many people dream of success and believe that success means becoming the chief executive, but few make it that far. For many of those who don't make it, their only reward is the dream. This book is not for dreamers. This book is for doers with a positive outlook and recognition of the nearly limitless potential before them.

FOLLOWERSHIP

My initial strategy when I went to work for Truett Cathy went something like this: "If I do the things Truett does not like to do, there might not be a limit to what he would be willing to pay me!" Getting ahead means doing what the boss does not like to do.

The gurus of leadership development will not suggest

that you do what the boss does not like to do. Instead, they encourage people to "lead from the front." But if everyone leads, everyone is going in a different direction. Moreover, if you jump in front of everyone, you have put your boss behind you. Charging ahead of your boss? Not a recommended career move.

Do you desire a satisfying career with opportunities for advancement in the future? The first step is to identify what the boss does not like to do. The second step is to find a way to do what the boss does not like to do, and exceed expectations. You will learn a lot about people, and a lot about yourself, in the process.

I chose to become a follower of Truett, and I quickly learned what he did not like to do. I discovered ways to get those things done to his satisfaction, or better—to exceed his expectations. As you read, think, and you will see that there is a difference between being a yes-man worker and a Creative Follower—a big difference. Being a follower is an active role requiring a great deal of creativity, personal initiative, and the ability to execute tasks with excellence.

This whole process begins with identifying a leader to follow.

A follower is someone who has chosen a leader.

LEADERSHIP

The word leader is not hard to understand, so let's keep the definition short, simple, and easy to remember: a leader is someone who has followers. Many authors and speakers devise complex formulas for defining leadership. Rather than clarifying the issue, however, lengthy definitions complicate and take away from a simple understanding of the simple idea.

A leader is someone who has followers.

UNIFYING PURPOSE

Followers are not attracted just to the leader. There are three connected parts to the leader/follower relationship. A follower is attracted to a leader because that leader has a vision, a purpose, a reason, a cause, or a goal that attracts the interest of the follower. Let's call this third part a unifying purpose. The leader also is able to communicate that purpose in a way that is inspirational, persuasive, and motivating to the follower. The unifying purpose is the basis of the relationship between the leader and the follower.

I was attracted to Truett Cathy as a leader, and I could picture myself in a satisfying role as his follower, helping him make his vision for Chick-fil-A a reality. Truett and I were joined together by a unifying purpose. We shared a vision of a chain of restaurants selling his Chick-fil-A sandwich.

The unifying purpose joins leader and follower together.

CREATIVE FOLLOWERSHIP

The idea of Creative Followership came alive when I began

to work for Truett. I learned how to put into practice the ideas that had been forming in my mind for a long time. Creative Followership is not an abstract theory or slogan; it is highly transferable and universal. Also, you should know that I did not create the idea of followership. I believe the ancient saying from Ecclesiastes: "There is nothing new under the sun." These ideas existed before I put them into practice. Yet, despite the thousands of books I have read in my lifetime, I have never found anyone advocating followership as the route to personal satisfaction and success. It took me years of real-life experience to reach this conclusion and the understanding of followership as I present it here.

More than a few readers likely will not be comfortable with the idea of being called a follower of anyone. There are certain unflattering implications connected with the word follower: conforming, docile, easily manipulated, weak, unable to succeed on one's own, or simply "not the leader." Our society values the leader above everyone else and promotes the notion of the alpha male or female as the ideal that everyone should strive to attain. We should be the top dog. We have been brainwashed to think of second place as no better than last place.

Yet, the stronger the leader, the stronger and smarter the follower must be to successfully support and execute the necessary tasks. It requires no less intelligence, strength, fortitude, or maturity to follow than it does to lead. The role of the follower is so much more than the role of an employee or worker.

WORKER

We must clearly understand the difference between the role of a worker and the role of a follower. A worker is someone who does a job. A worker is not a follower (though a worker could potentially become a follower). A worker works for a boss.

BOSS

A boss is the person with positional authority over workers. Being a boss has nothing to do with how well or how poorly a person does his or her job. All the word boss signifies is the person who oversees the activities of the workers.

LEADER/FOLLOWER/UNIFYING PURPOSE

Thus, you can see there is a difference between the role of the worker and the role of the follower, as well as a difference between a boss and a leader. The reason I can say that my career as a follower was successful and my job satisfying was that I chose a great leader. Truett Cathy had a strong, simple, and clear vision of what he wanted to accomplish, and I had a passion to help him make that vision a reality and to sustain it. Ours was a true leader/follower relationship. He had a purpose, and he communicated it simply and clearly, in a very inspiring manner. I understood the purpose and was able to communicate it to other followers and encourage them to accomplish it as well. The unifying purpose knit us together in a process of learning and working together to accomplish that purpose. Our working relationship was transformed from that of worker/boss to that of leader/follower.

CREATIVE FOLLOWERSHIP CANNOT BE TAUGHT

Even though Creative Followership is not something I can teach you, I can present to you the principles for your real day-to-day world of work and business. How you use these principles is up to you. No one needs to wait for a promotion, a corner office, or even a new job title. There is no reason to put this off another day. Start right where you are; the best time to start is now.

Reading this book will not teach you Creative Followership. It cannot be taught, because Creative Followership is about shaping your character. Only you and God can change your character.

You surely already know that who you are is more important than what you do, because who you are will determine what you do. The Greek sage and philosopher Epictetus said, "First say to yourself what you would be; and then do what you have to do." By choosing Creative Followership, you choose to begin a lifelong process of self-invention and reinvention.

Are you ready? Let's go.

CHAPTER 3

The Shadow

Shadows get a bum rap. Very young children who "discover" their shadow are fascinated. When you were very young, did you ever play a game that had something to do with your shadow, outside on a sunny day? Children make up games of all sorts about shadows. They especially like those that keep someone from stepping on their shadow.

When we reach adulthood, we often forget about the fun games we played as children, and we think of shadows in other ways. For an adult, the word shadow immediately conjures up all sorts of images; some of those images are gloomy and even frightening.

Ancient people feared shadows. They believed shadows turned into an extension of a man's soul or personality. They especially feared midday—the time when a person's shadow virtually disappears. Stepping on a shadow, they thought, could bring suffering upon the soul of its owner. They were literally afraid of their own shadows.

My use of shadow, however, has no relationship to anything dark or frightening. It is a metaphor describing the image and presence of a leader.

Like your visible shadow, the size and strength of your invisible shadow varies from person to person, yet everyone possesses this second shadow. This shadow may be good or bad, positive or negative, constructive or destructive. Before choosing a leader, check out the leader's shadow.

A person's shadow is made up of several components. These components will include, but are not limited to, the leader's integrity, ability, character, personality, and reputation.

An institution is the lengthened shadow of one man.
RALPH WALDO EMERSON

Tradition says that the Apostle Peter cast a long shadow. Families came from miles away to lay their sick on cots and pallets out in the street, positioned so that Peter's shadow would pass directly over them when he walked by (Acts 5:15). They believed Peter's shadow had such power that when it fell across someone ill, that person would be healed.

The role of Peter's shadow is difficult to explain, but one way or another, it possessed a great deal of power.

Another Peter—Peter the Great—is described this way by the Russian historian Nikolai Pogodin: "Everywhere we look, we encounter this colossal figure, who casts a long shadow over our entire past."

Encountering a worthy and powerful shadow can be a magnificent personal discovery. Potential followers must evaluate the shadow of a leader. What kind of a shadow does the leader cast? You have an obligation to yourself to choose between the many alternatives. Be diligent; avoid rushing to a decision. Becoming a part of the right shadow gives followers instant credibility they otherwise might not personally possess.

A powerful shadow enhances a follower's ability to actively participate in the unifying purpose. A trusted and established follower shares the reputation of the leader, as well as much of the leader's influence. Of course, with influence comes a great deal of responsibility. Effective use of the leader's influence depends on a dedicated trust/loyalty relationship between the leader and the follower.

Truett Cathy gave me a powerful shadow to work in. We built our relationship on my absolute loyalty to him and his unwavering trust in me, not on job descriptions. He knew I understood and could accurately communicate the unifying purpose to others. Therefore, my influence was in effect borrowed from Truett's influence. My ability to share in his reputation was a direct result of my working in the shadow of the leader.

A person with the gift of leadership and a broad sphere of influence casts a great shadow. After I came to the fundamental realization of Creative Followership, I deliberately joined forces with someone demonstrating the portrait and profile of a great leader. I had an image in my mind of the type of leader I could follow, even though in the beginning I could not explain it using these specific terms. I knew I would find success if I had the opportunity to be a creative follower in the shadow of greatness.

Here is how I conducted my search for a leader with a great shadow. Look for similarities with your own situation as we travel together.

CHAPTER 4

Fire Your Boss?

Lousy bosses are easy to spot. Perhaps no one has captured the essence of the lousy boss like cartoonist Scott Adams. Scott created the iconic pointy-haired boss (usually called the PHB) for his Dilbert comic strip, which portrays office politics and how it obstructs productivity in the workplace. The PHB is famous for his incompetence and total lack of concern for his fellow employees. This incompetent micromanager cares more about looking good in front of his superiors than communicating objectives. His human resources policies range from self-centered to purely evil. He is the ultimate example of a go-nowhere boss.

Do you currently have, or have you ever worked for, a boss like the PHB? If yes, I have some advice that may help.

Many people working for lousy or go-nowhere bosses see little chance of escaping the downward spiral of disrespect and lack of recognition. As a result, some feel unmotivated and do only what is necessary to keep their job. Others put the blame for the situation on the organization. They see the company promoting people who are good at managing projects but very poor in the role of supervising people. Ironically, a lot of people blame the problem on a lack of leadership training.

If you cannot stand your boss, you really should stop showing up at work day after day and doing nothing about the situation. My advice is always the same. Do one of two things: either get on board and support the boss or fire him. Yes, that's right. One of the options is to fire the boss!

WHY PEOPLE LEAVE JOBS

Notice I didn't say you must quit your job. I said fire your boss. People do not quit companies; they quit lousy bosses. Maybe, instead of moving out completely, you can just move around a bit. Get a transfer to another boss within your company, or as a last resort, find a new boss in another organization.

People do not quit companies;
they quit lousy bosses.

Sometimes employees know they are not appreciated, are not treated fairly, and have no hope of the situation getting better. There are bosses who reserve all rewards for their pals—those from their neighborhood, college, or club. Yet, some employees continue to put up with it. I don't understand that. Why would anyone continue to play at a table where the deck is stacked against you?

It is rather easy to miss the fact that workers are free to look for another job. Never consider yourself completely trapped in an employment situation, even though in tough economic times it may be more difficult and time-consuming to find another place to work. Fortunately, we live in a country with many options.

Another thing to consider is this: if someone leaves because he or she cannot stand the boss, the boss should be glad. The real problem develops when workers reject the boss's agenda but linger on anyway. A bad situation only gets worse when workers stay in a bad worker/boss relationship.

Can there be leadership that leads nowhere or toward nothing? Sometimes the boss may not appear to be moving the workers anywhere. Not moving usually means there is no goal line to charge toward, nothing to achieve, conquer, win, or improve upon. What a miserable situation that can be. Working for a boss with no purpose to bring people together, with no place to go or to be led, is what most people mean when they talk about a "dead-end" job—a fitting description for a job that isn't going anywhere. It is an unhealthy and unhappy place to work. And that lack of purpose falls squarely on the desk of the boss. Without a purpose, leadership is not taking place.

The *Gallup Management Journal*[1] published the results of a national survey that asked employees whether they would like to fire their boss. The results of the poll found that 24 percent of employees in the U.S. would fire their boss if they had the opportunity. Such opportunities are extremely rare; it is hard to imagine the circumstances in which a worker would have the power to terminate a boss. But there is another way to "fire" your boss: you can move, transfer, or leave.

It may be hard to see, and it may be a very difficult decision to make, but you really do have a choice. Remember that you have freedom because you are a voluntary worker. You may not have thought about workers in the same fashion as volunteers, but you are free to leave at any time. If you do not like your boss or his or her agenda, then find a new boss. Find a situation where you can be satisfied and successful. Fire your boss!

Let me share with you how I reached this conclusion and why I'm confident in giving out this advice: I followed it myself.

THE DAY I FIRED MY BOSS

Many years ago, after three bad boss situations in a row, I made the conscious decision that I would never again work for a lesser man than myself. This decision left me with two options. I could go into business for myself or I could find a

---

[1] http://businessjournal.gallup.com/content/28597/would-fire-your-boss.aspx.

better boss. I thought I could work for myself, so I chose to go that route first. Self-employment may be an option for you.

For me, self-employment was a character-building time of learning and gaining experience. My time as a commercial kitchen design consultant was complicated by the fact that my customers expected me to personally provide all the services. When I sent one of my employees out, the satisfaction level seriously decreased, but the more customers there were, the less time there was for me to devote to each one. This put a serious limitation on the growth potential of my business. For me, being a part of an organization with an opportunity for growth was very important. Therefore, although self-employment was an excellent learning experience, it lost its appeal when I finally faced the fact that the limited growth potential of my consulting business was never going to satisfy my long-term goals. That was the day when it dawned on me that I had to fire my boss. I fired myself.

THE PERFECT BOSS

Take a moment right now and pull up in your mind your image of the perfect boss. What does his or her picture look like? I do not mean physical attributes but character and personality. What personal qualities would you want this perfect boss to have?

Maybe you picture a strong, decisive leader who knows exactly what he or she wants. Perhaps you think of someone who invites suggestions, discussions, brainstorming, and direct input from workers. You may be thinking how nice it would be to have someone working closely with you, knowing exactly what is going on at every moment—or it may be that you work better with someone who is more distant from your day-to-day activities. Some believe that the perfect boss is concerned and cares about workers as people.

You may think something entirely different from anything mentioned here. There are as many descriptions of the perfect boss as there are worker personalities. We all have unique criteria; what one person thinks is the perfect dream boss may seem to another person a perfect nightmare. Being aware of this, you can better match your personality and preferences to the boss you choose for yourself.

You may wonder, "Does he really mean that we should choose our boss?" Yes! That is exactly what I mean. I not only think you should choose your own boss but I also am certain that this represents the very best method and approach to seeking employment.

—————— PRINCIPLE 1 ——————

Choose Your Boss

It is time we rethink the employment process. There is an entirely different way to look at it: rather than looking for a job, look for a boss. That's right—hire a boss. Look for someone with the character and traits you find desirable. Look for a leader with a purpose that is unifying and that you can share with the leader. You not only have a choice of career; you also can choose the person you work for. This is the first principle of Creative Followership.

Think about it. You select your friends, you choose your wife or your husband, you pick your doctor, and you prefer a certain dentist. In sum, you decide which individuals will fill vital roles in your life. Why not apply this same logic to your career by choosing your boss? You will spend a good deal more time with your boss than you will with your dentist! Be highly selective!

Here is a way to think about how you will look for a boss. We know eHarmony for its online matchmaking/dating services. According to their advertisements, if you want to find your soul mate, they can help. Simply fill out a personality profile, and for a fee, they will match the personality traits of your profile across what they call the 29 Dimensions of Compatibility—scientifically predicting and assisting you in locating the most compatible person for a successful long-term relationship.

I am not going to say anything one way or the other about the value of this online service; I only wish to point out there is nothing similar to an eHarmony-type service for finding a boss. You have to develop your own profile and rely on your personal resources. Nonetheless, I urge everyone to use a similar process to match your many personality dimensions to your own image of the perfect match in a boss. When I put the principle of choosing my own boss into practice, I started with just such a profile for my boss, listing the characteristics I was seeking.

By now, I hope you have given some thought to what you would look for in a boss. If you started looking for a boss today, what questions would you ask? What are the critical, nonnegotiable qualities on which you will not compromise? There is no definite list of questions I would recommend, because this is an individual quest, grounded in individual values and your field or specialty of interest. Before you begin, though, you should get a firm grasp on the process that will make your search successful.

What are the qualities you are seeking? What is important to you personally? What is really important to your career? Give careful thought to what you need to know about your potential employer.

Once you know the values and qualities you are seeking, do your research on specific individuals, not just the company or organization. Choosing a boss calls for persistence, insight, and careful investigation. You should interview and check into character references on your prospective boss.

THE CREATIVE FOLLOWER'S
FOUR CRITERIA FOR CHOOSING A BOSS

Here are the four requirements on which I was not willing to compromise in my search for the right boss. I consider these to be the primary four steps toward my career as a creative follower.

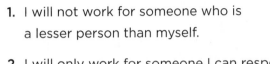

1. I will not work for someone who is
   a lesser person than myself.

2. I will only work for someone I can respect,
   look up to, and learn from—someone who
   can help me become a better person.

3. I will only work for someone who is building
   or growing something.

4. I will only work for someone who will let me
   express myself and make decisions,
   and who will value my input.

1. **I will not work for someone who is a lesser person than myself.**

I was serious about not working for someone who is a lesser person than myself. By "lesser" I do not mean an individual's financial, social, or educational status. Character was the critical issue. My standard of behavior would not permit me to work for someone who did not share the same standards I had disciplined myself to follow. As long as my boss met this criterion, I would not likely be asked to do something that was improper, illegal, or immoral. Someone who held the same standards as I hold would be incapable of crossing the line of good taste and judgment. If anything should ever turn questionable, due to oversight or not thinking through all the implications, there would be some assurance that my boss would not get angry with me for pointing out the discrepancy.

2. I will only work for someone I can respect, look up to, and learn from.

Second, I was determined to work only for somebody I could respect, look up to, and learn from, someone who could help me become a better person and grow professionally. Respect is something earned, not a feature of a title, office, rank, or position. One must demonstrate respect for people in authority—that is a given. But one also should show respect for all people, no matter their title, position, income, or any other factor.

Respect is one's desire to show honor, or a desire to demonstrate submissiveness to another. Submissiveness is a word seldom heard, but it is a great concept to understand and use. Submission means holding another person's wishes in such high esteem or regard that we gladly take the opportunity to help make those wishes come true. Furthermore, it means putting aside our own opinion or wishes and willingly adopting someone's agenda as if it were our own. I can only do something like this for a person I hold in very high esteem. To show submission for someone who is wrong, inexperienced, or not wise is not something I am willing to do.

Be true to yourself; find somebody you can honestly and earnestly respect in the way I have described. If I worked for a boss I thought knew much more than I did, I was certain I could profit by learning from him. You should leave work each day a little bit smarter and wiser, and an overall better person, just from being around the boss.

3. I will only work for someone who is building or growing something.

Third, I was not going to compromise my desire to work for someone who was building or growing something. I have always been particularly interested in the successful growth of organizations. I wanted to be where I could see growth every day. There is great pleasure in knowing that my efforts are contributing to positive results. People want to see the product of their work. This is true regardless of what product or service is at the end of the line. Furthermore, growth attracts outstanding people. I wanted to be a part of a growing organization and to work with outstanding people.

We all like to be a part of something that is bigger than we are. For me, that's very significant for career satisfaction. Even so, just being a part of something that is growing is not enough. You must be growing toward something constructive and for a purpose that sparks your enthusiasm. You need to do things you really enjoy. If these two ideas come together, I think all of us would say we want to be a part of something we enjoy doing but cannot accomplish alone.

4. I will only work for someone who will let me express myself and make decisions.

Last on the list—but far from least important—was the freedom to express myself, a key component of my requirements. Having people in the organization with innovative thoughts and diverse points of view contributes a great deal of value. The freedom to express myself and make my own decisions was an absolute and nonnegotiable criterion. Henceforth, I would only work for someone who would value my input.

Stay with me to see how I put my four Creative Followership criteria for choosing a boss into action and chose my last two bosses.

Choose Your Boss

CHAPTER 5

Finding
a New Boss

I t was September 10, 1968. Four years earlier I had successfully used the four criteria; I had fired my boss and
hired a new boss: myself. I was now a commercial kitchen and
restaurant design consultant, doing business as Food Service
Design, Inc. After four years I chose to fire myself. I reached
this conclusion because I was no longer satisfying criteria
number three: the consulting business was not growing.

I realized that, all around me, the food service industry
was growing at a phenomenal pace. The fast-food chains,
especially, were expanding rapidly, but my own business
had reached its growth potential. The time had come for me

fire my boss and find a new boss. There was no shortage of opportunities, but even though I had chased many leads and interviewed several potential new bosses, I had not found a single one that satisfied all four points of my criteria. Then, my search finally paid off.

THE PROCESS OF FINDING A NEW BOSS

One of my clients, Truett Cathy, was interested in me, and I was interested in him. Truett would be more than just a boss. He was already a recognized leader in both the restaurant industry and the community. He was a man I looked up to and respected, and he was growth oriented. Three points of my criteria would be fully satisfied. However, I had serious doubts regarding point number four—allowing me to express myself. Here is why.

A few years earlier, Truett had finalized his recipe for the original Chick-fil-A chicken sandwich. At that time, the only restaurant he operated was the Dwarf House in Hapeville, Georgia, but that Chick-fil-A sandwich sold so well that he quickly had more than 50 franchise agreements with independently owned restaurants to serve Chick-fil-A sandwiches as part of their menus. His product was attracting a lot of attention. The previous year, I had helped him draw up the plans for his first franchise restaurant based exclusively on serving Chick-fil-A. The location was in the first enclosed mall shopping center in Atlanta, Greenbriar Mall. That Chick-fil-A restaurant became a spectacular success.

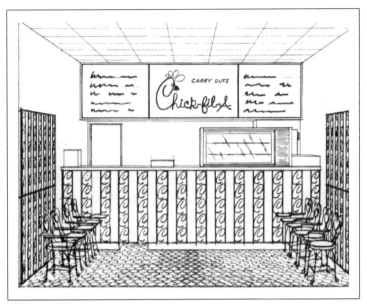

Original sketch of Chick-fil-A of Greenbriar Mall by Jimmy Collins

The customers were not the only ones interested in Chick-fil-A. Executives from the regional Morrison's Cafeteria chain were very enthusiastic about both the product and the new mall restaurant concept. They came forward and made an offer to buy out Truett. Truett was presented with a very attractive deal that included Morrison's purchasing the rights to Chick-fil-A and hiring Truett to stay on to help develop the Chick-fil-A concept.

Truett gave the offer serious consideration. He told me that, should he accept the offer, he wanted me to consider coming to work for him at Morrison's, to be in charge of design and construction. I told him I was not interested in working for

Morrison's, but that if he were to consider building Chick-fil-A on his own, I might be interested in working directly for him.

Truett understood the growth potential of Chick-fil-A and became more enthusiastic about the personal satisfaction he would derive from growing at his own pace and in his own style, rather than taking directions from Morrison's, even though the money they offered was very enticing. Truett declined their offer and developed his own vision of what Chick-fil-A would be.

When Truett decided to grow Chick-fil-A himself, he offered me a job to help him make his vision a reality. I asked for time to consider it. I needed time to review my four criteria and make sure this would work for me.

Truett was both a good business client and a good friend. We had known each other for ten years. I was sure he would be a good, perhaps even a great boss. I knew that joining him to build Chick-fil-A would be an exciting venture. Without a doubt, he would satisfy the first three points of my criteria. However, I had serious concern about point number four.

EXPRESS YOURSELF!

You will recall that my fourth criterion was, "I will only work for someone who will let me express myself and make decisions, and who will value my input."

I knew what expressing myself was like because I was able to express myself with many other clients. Most of my clients explained their needs and some conceptual ideas, gave me the menu, introduced me to their architect and interior designer, then turned me loose to design the kitchen and food service facilities. We all worked closely together, but I was responsible for the food service design.

My work for Truett was very different. Truett had hired me several times to design kitchens and restaurants for him. Although I thought very highly of him, we did not have the same type of relationship I had with most of my clients. My design process with Truett went like this: it was Truett's mind and my hands. Usually he came to my office, stood by my drafting table, and told me exactly what he wanted. He liked me to draw pictorial views of workstations and equipment and then combine them into the overall plan. This is how things went when I worked with Truett as a consultant, drafting the plans for the new building to replace the original Dwarf House and designing the first Chick-fil-A franchise restaurant in Greenbriar Mall.

Working with Truett on numerous projects had left me with serious doubts about whether I would be able to express myself fully. Would my input be valued? Would I be making decisions or just carrying out instructions? I was postponing my final answer while I kept wrestling with the decision.

Pleased with the success of the first Chick-fil-A mall restaurant, Truett hired me once again to help him design a second mall restaurant location, for the new Oglethorpe Mall in Savannah, Georgia. I drew up dozens of concept plans for this location, but he did not like any of them.

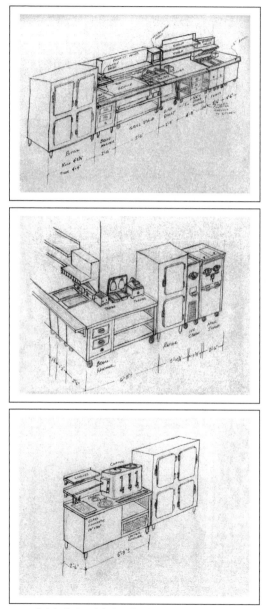

Original pictorial view drawings of workstations
for the Dwarf House by Jimmy Collins

However, I am not easily discouraged, and I kept trying to create the ideal plan for a quick-service restaurant that would fit in any of the new malls being built in every part of the country. I was excited about the latest plan I had drawn up for the new location. This time I was confident it would be exactly right for generating high sales volume in a shopping mall location. Finally, I was scheduled to show Truett my latest design. I also would have to give him an answer to his question about whether I would agree to work for him.

Unfortunately, I was not going to accept Truett's job offer. My wife, Oleta, and I had discussed and prayed about this decision. We had agreed that I would not go to work for Truett because it would not satisfy my fourth criterion.

As I arrived at Truett's office with the new plans neatly rolled up with a rubber band, the first thing he said was, "I need to know today whether you are going to come to work for me or not." Hoping to put that conversation off for the moment, I suggested, "Well, let's look at the plans first." He agreed.

As I was unrolling that rubber band, Truett asked me, "What do you think about what you have there?"

I stopped and answered confidently, "This is it; this is a winner."

I continued unrolling the rubber band, eager to share my new plan. When I was almost to the end of the roll, Truett spoke again. I stopped. He asked, "Are you sure?"

I said, emphatically, "Yes!"

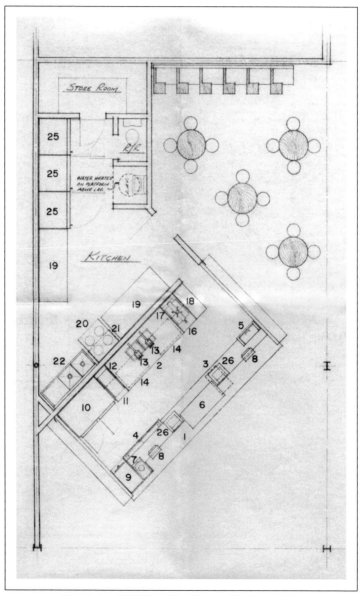

Original plan of Chick-fil-A of Oglethorpe Mall by Jimmy Collins

Chick-fil-A of Oglethorpe Mall, April 1969

He looked at the still-rolled-up plans and said, "Then that is what we will do."

I looked down and the rubber band was not quite to the end of the roll. The significance of that moment was suddenly clear.

ALL MY CRITERIA SATISFIED

Something important had changed. He *did* value my input! He would allow me to express myself and make my own decisions. My final objection to working for Truett instantly vanished; it was like receiving divine confirmation at the end of a long process of searching and praying. How easy it might have been to draw the wrong conclusion about Truett.

Then he asked me again, "Are you coming to work for me or not?"

"Yes!"

That is how the events unfolded. My four criteria were fully satisfied. I had found both a good boss and a great leader. It was September 10, 1968, and I was stepping into the shadow of greatness.

Principle 1, Choose Your Boss, is so critically important that I want to revisit it, now that you have more background information. I went looking for a boss who was also a leader, and I had specific required qualifications for that person—qualifications I would not compromise. You will perform your best when you have a boss who is a leader you can respect and follow. Choose your boss, but make certain that you choose your boss carefully. Pick the leader you want to follow, and then exercise care and thoughtful consideration when making the final decision. The right boss can be highly beneficial and can motivate you to perform feats you didn't know you were capable of accomplishing. If you choose the right leader and get on his or her train, you can ride a long, long way.

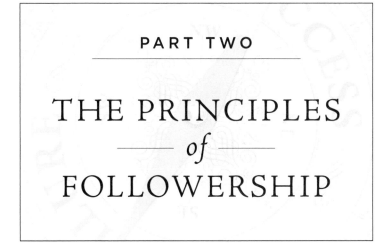

PART TWO

THE PRINCIPLES
of
FOLLOWERSHIP

CHAPTER 6

The Journey Begins

At the age of 12, I began my first job. Even then, the discovery of followership principles was slowly forming in my mind. By the time I went to work for Truett Cathy at age 32, they were developing into the principles that are the basis of Creative Followership. However, at that time I had not named them.

Even though my father worked two jobs, they were low-paying manual labor jobs, so he did not earn very much. Mother was a skilled seamstress; she made most of our clothes and sewed for other people to earn extra money. She also kept children for other mothers while they worked. All five of us children sought ways to contribute to the family's financial needs.

Before I was 12 years old, I earned money many different ways: cutting grass, raking leaves, collecting scrap metal and soft drink bottles (recycling is not a new idea), even picking cotton. My first job with scheduled working hours was at a neighborhood store, Brown's Grocery. Mr. John Brown hired me when I was 12 to deliver groceries and keep the store tidy. He provided a cycle truck—a heavy-duty bicycle with a small wheel and large basket in front and a regular-sized wheel in the rear. Many people in that neighborhood did not have automobiles in 1948.

To take full advantage of Mr. Brown's free delivery service, his customers either ordered groceries by phone or walked to the store to make their purchases. Then I delivered them.

I quickly discovered the income-enhancement potential of delivering groceries. I didn't just take the bags of groceries to the customer's door. I insisted on carrying them all the way to the kitchen. After I was in the kitchen, I would offer to put the groceries in the pantry or icebox (only about half of our customers had refrigerators). I liked those tips!

That grocery delivery job was an important learning experience for me. Right away I realized that the only reason Mr. Brown hired me was that he needed someone to do the things that he did not like to do. Mostly, that arrangement was okay with me because I enjoyed my work. I worked after school Monday through Friday and then all day on Saturday.

Saturday was the day Mr. Brown always sent me two blocks up the street to Lipham's Grill to buy his lunch.

Picking up the boss's lunch was not a problem, except on Saturday, when he always had a bottle of beer with his lunch. I did not like buying his beer! My parents and grandparents never drank alcohol. This was the first of many times when my work conflicted with my moral standards, the first of many confrontations with difficult choices. We all face difficult choices in the workplace, and how we choose to respond to them either builds our character or tarnishes our reputation.

Should I do what the boss told me? Should I refuse to carry beer back to the store and face the possibility of losing my job? The decision was not easy, because I needed that job. The risk was too great. So I complied and went to Lipham's, bringing back the boss's lunch, including the beer.

It was a hard lesson that still troubles me to this day. But it was the first installment of learning the importance of my first principle of Creative Followership—Choose Your Boss. You should read that as "choose your boss carefully." Thoughtful selection was not on my mind when I went to work for Mr. Brown; you could truthfully say I didn't carefully choose him as my boss. All I thought I needed was a job, and he was the first person who would hire me for a job with scheduled hours. Although I was no stranger to work, this job was the first one I considered a "real" job—one with a steady and predictable income.

When I went to my father for advice, he told me to keep the job while I looked for a better one. That is exactly what

I did. It took a few months but I found a job delivering the *Atlanta Journal* weekday afternoons and Sunday mornings. My new boss, Mr. Murphy, had only two absolute rules: arrive early on Tuesday afternoon to pay for the previous week's papers and do not cause any customer complaints.

This time I did not just get a job; instead, I did my research and asked other paperboys what the boss was like. I chose my boss and was satisfied to work for him for two years. My journey of followership was under way, even though I did not realize where it was taking me at the time.

BEGIN THE JOURNEY OF CREATIVE FOLLOWERSHIP

Previously, I mentioned that I cannot teach you followership but that I can share with you the principles of Creative Followership that worked for me. Creative Followership is a process. Start where you are, right now. Good boss, lousy boss, in-between boss—no matter. Be a dedicated creative follower right now, even if you are in the process of looking for a new boss. The practice will be invaluable in the future.

Many followers begin by being employed not as followers but as workers. Those initially hired as workers sometimes find they are won over by the urge to join up and follow the leader. Others may be drawn by the shared camaraderie around a unifying purpose and choose to become followers. These workers-turned-followers are people who see and understand the attraction of being in harmony with other followers around a common goal or purpose.

Creative Followership starts out incrementally, and then the process accelerates, but it must start somewhere. Here is the place to start.

By now I should have made it clear that a boss is someone with authority, whereas a leader is someone with followers joined to the leader via a unifying purpose. The difference between a boss and a leader is huge—do not overlook it. Suppose you are working for a boss who does not know what he or she is doing. You may be working for a boss with a failing grade on management. If you have a job now, you already know whether you have a good boss or a lousy one. If you have a lousy boss, I encourage you to think positively and realize that having a bad boss may be a good thing! That's right. You can still grow and develop professionally under the wing of a lousy boss. There is a positive way to look at virtually any situation.

LEARN FROM THE WORST BOSSES

Think through the logic of this with me. Working for a lousy boss means one is in a learning-rich environment. I learned from the worst boss I ever had, just as I did from the best ones, and so can you. You can learn many things quickly from the worst bosses, and you will get insights about how things should not be done. You certainly will learn more from the things happening to you than you learn from watching them happen to others. In fact, the more engaged or personally affected you are, the more lessons you will learn.

These firsthand negative experiences are not pleasant, yet they are excellent character-building opportunities. They are perhaps more valuable than the day-to-day lessons you could be learning from positive experiences, because you are more likely to retain what you are learning and to take the principles with you. The experience will make you a better person because you will walk away with determination not to repeat the boss's mistakes. You will have a foundation of understanding and personal wisdom that others will not have. Although it is not pleasant, it is true: a bad boss can be a good thing.

Having had several bad bosses along the way, let me tell you about my worst. For our purpose here, let's call him Mr. Smith. The married Mr. Smith was having an affair with the full-time check-out clerk at a small, old, run-down store that was part of a national supermarket chain. Besides having an affair with her boss, the clerk was stealing a lot of money from the store, and so were several other employees.

In a close work environment, there are no secrets. When things are not right, everyone knows. So everyone working at the store knew what was going on, knew who was cheating, knew who the thieves were, and was convinced that Mr. Smith was fully aware of it as well. Yet he did nothing. When you think about it, why would he care? He was already cheating on his wife with an employee; stealing probably would not have caused any real crisis in his conscience. And there I was, a part-time worker at age 17. I, Jimmy Collins, found myself in a really bad boss situation.

In 1953, in that old store located in a very low-income area of Atlanta, we did not have refrigerated produce displays. Crushed ice was put in galvanized steel display trays to keep the fruit and vegetables fresh. Because we were not open on Sundays, everything that would be salable on Monday had to be put in the walk-in cooler over the weekend. It was a weekly chore.

As the sun was setting on my first Saturday afternoon at work, Mr. Smith came to the produce section and started pointing. He said, "I want this, this, this, and that gone today."

I turned to an experienced employee and asked, "What does he mean?" He showed me.

At that time, produce was weighed by an employee, who calculated the price and wrote it on a brown paper bag that was then used to hold the fruit or vegetables. So, we weighed and bagged up the "this, this, this, and that;" marked prices on the outside of small brown paper bags; and proceeded to walk around the store dropping these in the carts of unsuspecting customers when they were not looking. If a customer at the check-out counter said, "This item is not mine," we would simply pick up the bag and drop it in someone else's cart, just repeating the process until it was all gone. At age 17, I did what the boss said. Later, when I was older and wiser, I would take a stand and refuse to do that sort of thing.

This is just one example of what went on in that store. Mr. Smith was an awful boss, but I learned a lot from him. A few months after I went to work there, however, the company closed the store and I was transferred to another store, with a good boss.

Something like my experience in that store tends to stick in one's memory. I have carried the lessons of my bad bosses with me all my life. Those lessons were very important later, when I was the boss. If you are working for, or ever find yourself working for a boss like Mr. Smith, you know what to do: learn all you can while you are looking for a boss who is a leader with a unifying purpose—the one you want to work for. Then fire that lousy boss and move on!

LEARN FROM THE BEST BOSSES

Suppose, though, that you have an excellent boss. Well, do not despair! You can also learn things from the best bosses, but it will be more difficult and will require more concentrated effort.

Watch with great care and observe the things a good boss does and how he or she does them. Anyone can remember when a boss does something wrong; therefore, you must be intentional in your observation, because good leadership is easy to take for granted. In fact, when we are in the presence of good leadership, we usually are not even aware of it. Everything goes so well that leadership seems unnecessary; it creates the illusion that everything is seamless and smooth.

The very best leaders make us feel as if we are in control. That is why we must deliberately and carefully study our good bosses. Good bosses are good because they operate from a set of principles that do not change and that apply equally to all levels of the organization at all times. Good bosses do not have a set of "what to do" rules. Instead, they have something more meaningful: "why to do" principles. These usually will not be a written list but will nonetheless be known and understood by everyone. The "why to do" principles not only support practices of what to do but also provide guidance for fair treatment of everyone under all circumstances.

PRINCIPLE 2
Know Your Boss

Whether she or he is lousy or great, learn about your boss. Do you want to be successful at work? You need to know your boss, learning all you can about his or her strengths, talents, likes, and dislikes. Figure out the boss's weaknesses. You will need to know these things in order to succeed personally and to help your boss succeed.

Ask questions as you go about your day. Find out what the boss likes to do. You should start by finding out what parts of her job she most enjoys and what parts she really dislikes. Watch closely and find out those things the boss does really well and those things she does not so well.

Then observe everything in between. It will gradually become apparent where the boss has strength and where the boss is a weak performer. After you have made your observations, compare your strengths to the boss's weaknesses. Where there is a match, utilize your skills in that area. Offer to help with a task that amplifies the boss's weaker areas—or just get the task done on your own. Don't be afraid to take some risk.

Know your boss.

————— **PRINCIPLE 3** —————
Do What Your Boss Does Not Like to Do

After you discover what the boss does not do well, you may be surprised to find that he probably would be glad to hand these things over to someone else. Soon after going to work for Truett, people would ask me what I did at Chick-fil-A. I would answer, "I do what Truett does not like to do." Moreover, if Truett was present he usually would follow that statement up with something like, "And I don't like to do very much." Truett was being both modest and humorous when he made that statement. That is what Truett would say; I would never have said that!

When I went to work for Truett, I studied him. I spent a great deal of time and energy learning him. I recommend that you do this with your boss. Apply Principle 2: Know Your Boss. Why? Because it suits your new (or renewed) role and highest priority: doing the things that your boss does not like to do. Truett is a highly motivated, hardworking, and committed individual, but like everyone, there are things that he would prefer to have someone else do for him. This is how we forged a partnership built around a common objective. I was thinking, "If I do what Truett does not like to do, I can add value to Chick-fil-A." This is what you can do with your boss, and if he or she is successful, you will be too.

Early on, Truett let me know his intentions and expectations for me. He said, "I want Chick-fil-A to grow, but I don't want problems. With years of working double shifts in a 24-hour restaurant, I have had enough problems to last a lifetime." After learning that, it occurred to me, "If I take care of his problems, there may be no limit to what he might pay me." Since I am highly motivated by financial reward, I was sure I had discovered a pathway to my personal success and satisfaction—Principle 3: Do What Your Boss Does Not Like to Do.

Because I did what Truett did not like to do and handled his problems, my influence grew, both inside and outside Chick-fil-A. In addition, I was most pleased to learn that my compensation did grow accordingly. I can confidently advocate this principle. It transfers to nearly any leader/follower situation I can think of. It will be up to you to apply it.

Do what your boss does not like to do.

BE THANKFUL FOR A DO-NOTHING BOSS

When I was teaching Chick-fil-A franchise restaurant employee supervision training classes, I liked to ask this question: "Do you work for a boss who does not like to do much?"

Usually, after a hesitant glance around the room, everyone would eventually say yes.

My next question always surprised the listeners. I would ask, "Do you realize how fortunate you are? Just think of the opportunity this leaves open for you."

In most classes, someone would say, "How about me? My boss does not like to do *anything*!" And I would tell him, honestly, "Your opportunities are unlimited."

I was not being sarcastic; this is a true statement. An inexperienced worker may not realize that a leader will leave a follower a lot of opportunities to express himself. A worker will shirk the responsibility and wait for instructions. A follower, on the other hand, will grab the opportunity and run with it.

It amazes me when employees spend time complaining about a boss who does not work. It is astonishing because what people usually mean is that the boss is not joining them in doing the kind of work the employees are paid to do. The boss has a different job than the workers, and the boss should not be doing the same job as the workers. There may be times when employees think the boss is doing nothing when they compare it to what they are doing. The boss may have a job that looks easy—or it may be a job you would not want if you had it—but none of that really matters. There are times when a good boss will step in to help employees at critical moments, but employees should realize that if a boss is duplicating the tasks the workers are doing, then the boss is neglecting the job the boss is being paid to do. In this situation, a follower will help the boss get back to her leadership position, doing her own work.

——————— PRINCIPLE 4 ———————

Do What Your Boss Does Not Do Well

All of us sometimes find ourselves doing and trying to do things we don't do well. If doing things we don't do well were an option, we could just avoid doing those things and forget about it. Most of us, including your boss, do not have that option.

What's the best way to make the boss look good? Identifying and completing, with excellence, those things the boss does not do well. Use your strengths to build on the boss's weaknesses.

Consider this personal example. When I was in the sixth and seventh grades at Central Park Elementary School, I remember learning a valuable lesson. At recess the boys usually played softball, and we had an unusual rule: after two strikes, a batter could choose someone to take the next pitch. If your substitute batter hit the ball, you were permitted to run the bases.

I am not athletic so I liked that rule. When I used it, I always got on base. My choice for a substitute hitter was easy: I always chose Harry Blondheim. Harry was the best athlete in my school, and I was happy to tap into and benefit from his talent. A few years later he became a star basketball player at the University of Georgia.

The valuable lesson from the elementary school playground was clear and has stuck with me for the rest of my life: you'll never strike out if you pick the best player to step in at the right moment. Pick the best to make things happen when you need help. I have practiced that principle from that day forward.

With that pick-the-best-player idea in mind, it occurred to me that this might also work if the better player initiates the substitution. What if I know beyond any doubt that I can do something better than my boss? Can I just step up to the plate and get it done? If there were things I could do better than my boss, why not just do those things for him? I decided to try it.

I was very cautious about how I positioned it. My approach was to mention that if I did for Truett the things he did not do well (no, I will not say what those things were), it would free him up to do more of the things that he did really well. He was receptive to the idea.

When two or more people are working together, it is important to divide the work so everyone can achieve their maximum performance for the greater good of both the project and the organization. You and your boss must divide tasks and put your time and energy toward what each of you does best. When both you and your boss are doing what each of you does best, your organization's performance will soar, as will your personal performance and satisfaction. Coordination of effort pays off, and it may be up to you to respectfully and diplomatically initiate this division of labor. When you practice Principle 4: Do What Your Boss Does Not Do Well, your persistence and patience in working out the details will be worth the effort.

Do what your boss does not do well.

— PRINCIPLE 5 —
Do Not Compete
with Your Boss

I vividly recall one afternoon when I returned to the office after speaking at a Kiwanis club luncheon. I saw Truett and told him what a fine reception I had received, thinking he would be pleased by the positive emotional connection I had created for Chick-fil-A among those present at the luncheon.

Though he was usually predictable, his reaction that day was not what I had anticipated. He said, "You could get a speaking engagement every day. All organizations have someone responsible for finding speakers." At that time, Truett was averaging two speaking engagements per week. He went on, "You leave the speaking to me and concentrate on the business."

Truett likes to speak and he is an excellent communicator. By putting myself out there as a public speaker, I had violated my own principles 3 (Do What Your Boss Does Not Like to Do) and 4 (Do What Your Boss Does Not Do Well). That day I added my fifth Creative Followership principle: Do Not Compete with Your Boss.

From that day forward I did not accept a business-oriented speaking engagement. I knew that Chick-fil-A only needed one figurehead speaker. I focused on the business and left the speaking to Truett.

I chose to step back out of the spotlight and into Truett's shadow. As a follower, this is a decision you will be called upon to make from time to time. You will need to determine what is in your best interest. Are you prepared to venture out on your own? Are you prepared to find a new boss? Is it better to work in the shadow of your leader? I was convinced that my future was brighter in Truett's shadow.

The follower must never put himself in competition with the leader. Remember your role as the follower; your role is to work for the boss, not against the boss or in competition with the boss. No matter how tempting it may be to draw attention to yourself, the competition is fixed; you will not come out the winner. Just continue to remind yourself of the larger picture and why you do what you do—you have chosen a boss to stand behind and support. The more you promote the boss, the more success you create for the boss, the more you succeed as well. Get on the right train and it will take you where you want to go.

Do not compete with your boss.

Make Your Boss Look Good

At the risk of being redundant, I want to emphasize that the follower should always practice this principle: make your boss look good. As we proceed through the followership principles, you will see many ways to make your boss look good. Don't hesitate! Do it! If you keep working to make your boss look good, your boss will continue to advance in the organization. Your boss will protect you and provide you with the materials and resources that you need to keep supporting him or her. In the event that you have a boss who is not smart enough to see that you are helping him to accomplish his tasks, remember Principle 1: Choose Your Boss!

You are a volunteer. Do the best you can to make the boss look good where you are, even if you are actively engaged in the process of choosing a new boss.

If you are seeking a new boss within your organization, those with authority over your boss are probably very familiar with your boss's strengths and weaknesses. If your boss has a sudden surge in talent or a brand-new skill set the people in charge have never seen before, they will notice. It is very likely they also will notice the true source of talent, and your actions will stand out against the background of what your boss did in the past. But avoid any temptation to help the process of discovery along. Think about the risk of undermining and competing with the boss. These things get one fired, not promoted.

If you are seeking a position with a new organization, re-member that it is easier to get a job when you have a job. Doing the best you can and maintaining a standard of excel-lence is the wisest route to keeping yourself employed. While you are still there, remember to learn all you can!

Make your boss look good.

After all that has been said, you know that I am not ad-vocating mindless acceptance of all that the boss says, if you believe the boss has made a poor decision. After you have shared your point of view, accept and support the outcome— barring anything illegal, immoral, or in violation of policy. You should of course not be working for someone whose ac-tions contradict good moral judgment.

CHAPTER 7

Mustangs and Mules

PRINCIPLE 7
Take Responsibility

I want to point out something important that I have never read anywhere and no one ever told me: It is not important that I be given very much authority on the job. Authority is nice to have, but there's no point in worrying about how much your superiors grant you in your job description.

Am I correct in assuming that you would like to have more authority at work? And that you are ready to take on more responsibility? Authority properly used comes packaged with responsibility. Therefore, as I discovered over the years, more authority can be gained just by taking responsibility. In this way, you can assume authority in bits and pieces. I gained more authority without having it given to me; all I had to do was figure out what the boss didn't like to do, take responsibility, and do it.

Take responsibility.

——————— PRINCIPLE 8 ———————

Everyone Likes Problems

Truett Cathy always says he does not like problems. What he really means is that he wants to choose his problems; he wants to decide which ones to deal with personally and which ones he wants fixed or prevented for him. We are all like that. We all have things we prefer to do ourselves and other things we do not really want to take up our time, so we can invest our time in something that is more enjoyable, interesting, or productive, something only we ourselves can do. True, some problems overwhelm, irritate, or just wear us down. But there also are problems that are more like an adventure. These are the ones we love to solve.

What was the most fun problem you ever solved or the most difficult challenge you ever conquered? Perhaps it was landing a huge fish or closing the biggest deal you ever made. Regardless of the setting, it can be exciting and personally challenging to achieve a victory over something that requires body and mind in a coordinated effort to achieve a desired result. With a little adjustment in one's perspective, a problem can seem a lot less like an obstacle to annoy us, and more like an opportunity to demonstrate skills and talents when we turn things around.

I saw my boss's desire to choose his problems as a wonderful opportunity. All I had to do was figure out what he did not like to deal with and then simply do what was necessary to fix it. Walking away from the events, I would have his appreciation and the new level of authority I wanted. In this manner, I did not need to ask for more authority. I just earned it piece by piece as I went along. The more things I could identify as problems the boss did not like to deal with, the more pieces I had to work with.

Everyone likes (to choose his) problems.

PRINCIPLE 9
Do Not Hoard Authority

You may be thinking, "That process could not go on forever. There are only so many hours in the day. I cannot do all of my work plus all the things the boss does not like to do, as well."

First, let me assure you that there is no need to worry about your plate becoming too full to handle. Once you begin to gain authority through Creative Followership—did you catch that?—once you begin to gain authority through Creative Followership, you will discover others who would like to pick up some of the pieces of your work. Never fall for the temptation to hoard your tasks. The only way you can add things to your plate is if others remove something from your plate. I found that other people were coming and gladly taking pieces of my job away. This step, Principle 9, is one that far too many people are not willing to permit, because they are not secure enough in their own abilities to continue the process into the future.

TERRITORIALISM

Territorialism is something that not only wastes resources and kills the spirit of cooperation but also holds hoarding individuals back and prevents their own growth and advancement. I loved my work; it was always changing. And that is another key to enjoyment and satisfaction in your career. Let capable people take pieces away; do not mark off territory.

Because I did enjoy my job, other people thought they might like to do what I did. I did not mind seeing others take things away from me, especially if it was a task I did not enjoy doing. Some of those tasks I really liked to do, but I let someone with more time, and in certain instances greater ability, accomplish that specific task.

This synergism of tasks evolving and revolving around is a good thing for everyone, and it is extremely healthy for the organization. The process of movement and dynamic change or constant motion is a positive for growth and innovation. We can grow and evolve as individuals when we get new responsibilities and when old responsibilities become new tasks in someone else's hands. It is never good to have people in the organization who get tasks or responsibilities and hang on to them at all costs.

Some people feel threatened by anyone who has taken a piece of their job away. Instead of recognizing an opportunity to move on to new and more challenging tasks and potentially more authority, they do whatever is necessary to repossess a task, defending their perceived territory. Territorialism is poisonous to productivity and benefits no one—especially the fence owner. Avoid territorialism! Learn to see beyond what you think and feel is your plot of land and learn to look up to the horizon and see the vast uncharted territory of new opportunity. If you think about it, everyone has only a 24-hour day and a seven-day week. If you want to move forward, then something you do now has to go to make room for that new thing.

WHEN YOU GO TOO FAR

Therefore, if you want more authority, take it; if you want a piece of the business, take it. Actually, my words usually went like this: "If you want a piece of my work, take it and run with it and do something productive with it." However, I must warn you that the simple act of taking it and running with it does not mean the boss will necessarily like what you have done. Always remember Principle 11: Do It the Way the

Boss Likes It Done, which we will cover later. This key component in successful Creative Followership is easily missed.

Sometimes you will go too far, overstepping the boundaries or doing the wrong thing. It is unavoidable. However, when that happens you should not slow down. Just find another way to do it so the boss will like it. This is something I cannot teach others how to do, because each situation is unique. I learned through the process of trial and error, which is something everyone must experience. Learn from each experience how to do better next time, but you must keep trying. The learning and trying of new things is part of the adventure; you must embrace the process and participate to the fullest. This is the only way to fully experience the greatest benefits of Creative Followership.

Do not hoard authority.

─────── PRINCIPLE 10 ───────
It Is Better to Restrain Mustangs than Kick Mules

At Chick-fil-A, I constantly reminded people, "It is better to restrain mustangs than kick mules." By "mustangs," I mean the people who live and work on the edge of their authority and occasionally beyond. "Mules" are those who reluctantly and stubbornly plod the same path and require constant pushing. It is true that mustangs do occasionally go too far—

some of them will often go too far. But which would you rather work with? Would you prefer working with people who possess initiative that you might occasionally have to restrain or people you must constantly prod and push? Which are you, a mustang or a mule?

In 1996, Rudy Martinez, a former hourly restaurant employee, became the Operator (franchisee) of a very poorly performing Chick-fil-A restaurant in South Park Mall, San Antonio, Texas. He was sure that he would make a winner out of a situation that had been an underperformer for ten years. Three months after he took control, I went to visit him, along with his consultant from our field staff. As we parked the car at the mall, the consultant said to me, "Jimmy, I need to tell you something you may not like. Rudy is selling some unauthorized items on his menu." This was a serious concern to the consultant because no Chick-fil-A Operator is to change the menu without approval.

Rudy had added chicken tacos to the breakfast menu. He said sausage biscuits, our most popular breakfast item at the time, did not sell to his clientele, but the breakfast tacos his wife made were attracting new customers. When I tasted them I understood why. I told Rudy, "If selling breakfast tacos can help you make a winner out of this restaurant, go for it."

He did make a winner of that store, and he earned a new Ford automobile by reaching his Symbol of Success sales goal—Chick-fil-A's highest sales performance recognition for Operators (always capitalized within Chick-fil-A, as

Truett Cathy, Rudy and Petra Martinez, Jimmy Collins

a sign of respect). Rudy earned it two years in a row. As you can guess, however, Rudy sold a lot more than breakfast tacos to achieve that level of sales.

Rudy Martinez exemplifies my concept of a mustang. He is willing to live out on the edge of his authority and even occasionally exceed it to reach his goals. He is not afraid to take risks. He is not easily discouraged. He will let nothing hold him back from finding the path to his goal.

By the way, in case you haven't noticed, breakfast burritos are now on the menu of the Chick-fil-A restaurant near you.

Ask yourself this question: How many positive changes that occur in organizations are brought about by mustangs? The answer: All of them! Do you see why I would rather restrain mustangs than kick mules?

It is better to restrain mustangs than kick mules.

Do It the Way the Boss Likes It Done

I am a mustang, and there were countless times I took things a little too far or a little too fast. I vividly recall a time when I decided to put a new process in place. Everything was moving along great—that is, until Truett heard about it. He immediately did not like it and he said so.

"I don't like it," he said. "I don't agree with it and you can just go undo it."

It was time to do exactly what the boss wanted. With some help from a few other people, things went back to the way they were before. However, do you think that stopped me from being innovative? No way! Was I upset; did I quit trying? No, I did not! Did it take away my initiative to keep trying? Not in the least!

What it did do was teach me a very valuable lesson. It taught me to be sure that what I did was more consistent with the boss's preferences. I had to learn to practice Principle 11: Do It the Way the Boss Likes It Done. It forced me to do my homework. It was my responsibility to know how my boss liked things done. I had to dig a little deeper and observe much more closely.

Making a mistake should never stop you from using your creativity or initiative, either. It is a learning process of trial and error. Mistakes help us make necessary corrections for future successes.

By the way, when I repackaged that rejected process and implemented it in a way Truett liked, I received his endorsement and support. Later, I will go into more detail on repackaging ideas.

Do it the way the boss likes it done.

Taking risks and making things happen can transform your work from mundane and boring to exciting and adventurous. People who complain about sameness in their job are bored for one reason: they have not made anything new and exciting happen. It is up to you to use your brain, shake things up a little bit, and keep things moving. Imagine how stagnant an organization would become if no one ever tried anything new, no one created on his or her own, no one took any initiative, no one ever took a little bit of someone else's task list but just did what was written in the job description. Not only would it be boring to work for that organization but also that organization probably would not grow and thrive. Change must be driven, and the drivers are the risk takers. Sometimes they get into trouble, but they are recognized and rewarded when they bring innovation and succeed.

PRINCIPLE 12

Let Others See the Boss in You

My goal was to support my boss in such a way that whatever I did was what the boss would have done. Yet I never tried to give my actions more weight by using the boss's name. When things did not go right, I never blamed the boss. I took responsibility myself and went to work to do whatever was necessary to correct the situation. Others never knew whether a decision was Truett's or mine. Even when we were not in complete agreement, I never positioned my action on something we were doing by saying, "Because this is what the boss wanted." Furthermore, I did not tell anyone when Truett overruled me. Those times when I was overruled were no one else's business; they were between Truett and me alone. Likewise, when I disagreed with Truett on something, I never disclosed these private interactions. There was much more to gain by keeping them close to the vest—and there was potentially everything to lose by recklessly discussing them with anyone else.

The objective was Principle 12: Let Others See the Boss in You. This was not because I could not make decisions or act independently. It was to present unified purpose and action. When the people in the organization see management in unity, they are more confident in their own roles. They know that management is in harmony and feel empowered to follow management's example.

Your work should mirror the quality and character of the boss. I do not think I need to explain every detail of how to do this. It is another instance where every situation is unique. If you have what it takes to be a creative follower, you can certainly work it out. If you have picked a leader you can follow, I assume you have picked a boss of excellence. Do things in a manner that will meet and even exceed your leader's personal standard. When you can do this proficiently, you have assumed an indispensable role for the leader. You have moved beyond just being a worker to being a follower of your leader.

By now, I hope you have forgotten the depiction of a follower as someone led mindlessly around by someone else. Far from being a demeaning, subservient role, followership places the creative follower in a position to greatly profit from the relationship professionally, personally, and financially.

He who tends the fig tree will eat its fruit,
And he who cares for his master will be honored.
KING SOLOMON (PROVERBS 27:18)

The follower who has made the boss look good and has done the things the boss does not like to do—or does not do well—eventually finds herself in a position to influence where the whole organization is going.

Let others see the boss in you.

—————— **PRINCIPLE 13** ——————
Help Your Boss Succeed

One of the marks of great leaders is the responsiveness and demeanor of the followers. The fundamental decisions made by a leader have a direct effect on the life of the organization. Outstanding people with keen insight and sound judgment surround great leaders. Therefore, followers must be willing to invest their future in the creative execution of decisions made by the leader. Creative Followership involves visible and affirmative support of the boss's decisions.

The creative follower has a huge role in the success of the leader. Help your boss succeed. This is the reason you were hired!

Do you know the vision for the future of the organization in the mind of the boss? You should! If you don't and you are listening, you may need a new boss. The next part is easy: after you know what the vision looks like, tailor your actions to support the boss's plans for the future.

Help your boss accomplish what he or she wants to do, consistent with the boss's personal preferences, point of view, and goals. Assist and support the message the leader is trying to communicate to other employees. Make sure everything you do not only lines up and strengthens but also breaks down barriers to the success of the leader's plans.

When Truett employed me in 1968, his initial assignment included two parts. First, "Help me open restaurants," and second, "See that they stay open." In an industry in which 59 percent of independently owned restaurants fail during the first year and 75 percent fail within five years, staying open is a challenge. There was a great deal of emphasis on the words "stay open."

Truett Cathy is a confirmation of Warren Bennis's observation about leaders: "They all have the ability to translate intention into reality and to sustain it."[2] Truett's intention was to build a business that would last, and it was clear that the longevity of the restaurants was very important to him. Making this a priority was critical to my career. It was what he had hired me to do.

Opening restaurants was the easy part. Anyone can do that. All you need is money. The difficult part of my assignment was to see that they stayed open. I considered it my make-or-break mission. I was determined to keep those restaurants open.

I know that most restaurant failures are just a matter of time, beginning the day they open. By being careful and thorough in site selection, lease negotiation, design, marketing, and cost control, we would only open restaurants with the best potential of staying open. Then, by devoting effort, energy, and resources to building customer satisfaction and sales, we would ensure that they stayed open. We were committed to building a chain of restaurants that would make Truett's vision a reality.

So, I urge you to be known for your passion and loyalty,

[2] Warren Bennis and Burt Nanus, *Leaders: Strategies for Taking Charge* (New York: Harper and Row, 1985), 226.

for helping the leader translate his or her vision into reality. This is how a vision becomes your unifying purpose. Choose the right boss and do this and you are bound to go places you never dreamed!

In addition, beyond the creative follower's individual commitment to supporting the leader, it is also the follower's role to assist the leader in gaining the support of others. The creative follower must assist the leader in spreading and clarifying the unifying purpose, completing projects, and reaching intermediate goals that support the unifying purpose.

Help your boss succeed.

— PRINCIPLE 14 —
Build Support in Advance

To effectively support your boss, you must be able to win the support of others, whether within or outside your organization. There will be times when some of the people you want to encourage to support your boss will rank higher in the organization or will be outside your usual area of influence. That is why it is so important to practice building support in advance. Use this skill when building support for your boss, or use it when building support for your own purposes. It works for either.

Suppose you are working with a committee, board, or any group that is to make a joint decision. It is important to get multiple opinions and views out in the open for discussion so that everyone has an opportunity to consider them carefully. If you are presenting an idea or proposal that requires the support of several people or departments, it is always good to use a process of building support and buy-in before the meeting. Responsible people in key positions do not like to be blindsided. They may be able to make important contributions to the matter under consideration if they have an opportunity for advance preparation. Alternatively, they may have valid reasons for rejecting the idea. You need to know those reactions in advance.

Many times I have seen people make surprise presentations at meetings because they were afraid they would not get an affirmation if certain key people knew about their proposal in advance. That is a very foolish approach and usually leads to failure, unnecessary embarrassment, and chaos.

Here is an example. Many years ago, when I was elected to my church board, I had several people caution me about one member of the board, the finance committee chairman. They said he was a stickler for detail; he wanted every i dotted and every t crossed. He was a certified public accountant, a very thorough and detail-conscious man. In addition, Charlie Pyke had grown up in a Salvation Army family and hated to see "the Lord's money wasted."

When I discussed with other members of my committee an idea I had, they said, "You'll never get that past Charlie."

Well, I respected Charlie. I was not alone; everyone respected and liked Charlie. He was a man who never met a stranger. When he spoke, he didn't play word games; you knew exactly where he stood on every issue. Charlie was my kind of guy!

I went to Charlie and asked him to help me evaluate what I was thinking about, to point out any weaknesses or potential problems. He had some excellent suggestions that I incorporated in my proposal before I presented it to the board.

The committee member who gave me the warning was correct. I didn't get it past Charlie. I got more than that: I had a better proposal than my original, plus Charlie's full endorsement and support. As a matter of fact, I always enjoyed Charlie's support because I valued his very wise input. I absolutely respected Charlie.

From this incident and many others, in all kinds of similar situations, I found that building support in advance works best. It shows respect for the contribution of the key players and promotes goodwill in general. It reduces dissent and helps avoid rejection. When I present a proposal, I aim for total support, and lining up support ahead of time is one way to better ensure that you and your boss are successful.

Whether you are working on behalf of the boss, your committee or board, or yourself, build support in advance. To fully and successfully support your boss, bring others along with you, approach them one by one with respect. This is how creative followers support their leaders.

Build support in advance.

CHAPTER 8

Effectively Using Input and Feedback

B efore joining Chick-fil-A, when I worked as a restaurant and commercial kitchen design consultant, I was most satisfied if, after a facility was finished and operating, a client said, "This is everything I expected it to be. Thank you for your help."

I enjoyed being a consultant. I listened carefully to my clients, they told me what they wanted, and then I just designed what they said they wanted. Sometimes it was rather challenging to accurately interpret their instructions and then translate that vision into a reality. There were so many aspects to keep in mind, including how to repackage all their ideas and make them fit the available space, time, and budget.

My experiences in the consulting business became very helpful in learning to practice Creative Followership. In consulting I had to gather input and feedback, interpret, translate, and repackage ideas for my clients; as a creative follower I learned that the same thing works for the leader I choose to follow.

——— **PRINCIPLE 15** ———

Gather, Interpret, Translate, Repackage

Seldom—and if my memory serves me correctly, maybe never—did my boss present a fully thought-out idea, packaged and ready to use. I had bosses who had many good ideas, but they usually needed to be finished and packaged. Some of their ideas were a little less than good, but by translating the rationale behind the ideas, I could repackage and present them in a better way.

The four steps of Principle 15 are not typically a part of anyone's job description; they are usually accomplished by someone who simply takes the initiative to get it done. Clearly, doing this should be a top priority for anyone savvy enough to see the value he or she might bring as a creative follower. A creative follower's role is a challenging adventure and involves the critical tasks of gathering, interpreting, translating, and repackaging the boss's ideas. When a creative follower succeeds at this, his reward is the recognition and appreciation of a satisfied leader, the respect of productive followers, and a strong reinforcement of the unifying purpose for all within the organization.

The creative follower helps answer the questions everyone asks: "How do I fit in to this new initiative? What is expected of me?" The creative follower has a key role to play in making things happen as the leader envisions them. To be prepared to play this role, however, you must genuinely know what is going on within the organization. Be hands-on in your approach, yet avoid the impression of micromanaging others.

Know and understand the unifying purpose, know and understand the boss, then learn to understand your coworkers. Focus on assimilating information from all facets of the organization. I will share with you the ways I learned to find out what is going on and how I learned to gather, interpret, translate, and repackage this information.

GATHERING INFORMATION

Before I retired from Chick-fil-A, people outside the organization often asked me about the business. When my reply to a question was, "I don't know," the response of surprise was often, "Don't you know what goes on at Chick-fil-A?"

You might be wondering why I would say I didn't know what was going on at Chick-fil-A, after I just encouraged you to know what is going on in your organization. In fact, my reply to this question continued: "I know *some* of what goes on at Chick-fil-A." I said that because the reality was it was neither necessary nor possible for me to know everything. I tried to focus on what was important for me to know. I gathered the most important information first.

Before determining what was most important, I had to ask myself, "Do I really know what is going on?" The most credible process for gathering information is to listen to feedback. Feedback is critical information about others' reactions to a project, a product, or someone's performance of a task. There are two kinds of feedback: positive and negative. Positive feedback is easy to get. It flows naturally to the boss because almost everyone is eager and willing to share it. Negative feedback is more difficult to get and almost everyone is reluctant to deliver it. No one wants to be the bearer of bad news. People are leery of delivering bad news because they are afraid of being labeled a complainer. As a result, the boss is usually the last person to learn about a problem.

After I retired, I was a regular customer in a local chain restaurant. The manager knew that even in my retirement I was willing to meet with folks and discuss challenging restaurant management issues. He asked me to meet with him, so I did. As we sat down I pointed out that the installation of his replacement booths had not been finished, even though the booths had been in place for several months. He told me that the design and construction department knew about it but they had never sent anyone back to finish the work. When I asked if he had called to remind them, he replied,

"They know about it." I told him they probably had forgotten about it and it was time to call again. He said, "Oh, no. I don't want to be known as a complainer."

Then he told me that his customers didn't like the chain's new bold-flavored coffee. In fact, I had recently heard several customers complain about the coffee. I asked whether he had reported this to his home office. Again he replied that he didn't want to be known as a complainer. I asked him, "What *do* you want to be? How about being known as a customer advocate?" He never asked me to meet with him again.

Situations like this are detrimental not only to workers, but also to customers and the organization. Those incomplete booths speak. They give first-time customers a bad impression; to repeat customers they shout out the restaurant's and the chain's lack of concern. Coffee that is disliked by so many but doesn't change in a timely fashion makes customers wonder why it takes so long to replace it with something less offensive to their taste buds.

If the problem for this manager is unwarranted shyness and timidity, he is not fulfilling his management role. If there is an unwelcoming or hostile response from higher up the chain of command, he should find a new boss. Both types of barriers to negative feedback undermine organizational effectiveness. As a creative follower, you will need to learn to identify and interpret lack of negative feedback as well as unrealistic positive feedback. Getting accurate negative feedback takes extra effort, but that is how you really find out what is going on.

It is impossible to fix a problem if you don't know a problem exists. You must find ways of effectively discovering problems. Access to reliable, up-to-the-minute information gives you an opportunity to learn what is going on and to make corrections before a problem spreads. You have to be proactive in seeking out those problems. I knew that my value as an effective creative follower was enhanced if I could identify problems and solve them as soon they happened—or even better, before they happened.

INTERPRETING

Interpreting is the process of understanding and being able to explain what someone says. The creative follower will learn to interpret the critical information of input and feedback so that it can be understood with clarity. Interpretation flows between the leader and the followers, and between the organization and the customer.

Sometimes specifics are challenging, because many leaders see things from a big-picture-only perspective. They see the overall goal, but the specifics of how to get where they want to be is usually worked out by the followers. From different places within the organization there are different perspectives; people see through lenses with different shades of color representing their department or area of responsibility. Different viewpoints create gaps in correctly understanding the motives, intentions, and true purpose of ideas. The potential for misunderstanding is very high; therefore, the creative follower becomes a valuable asset to the organization when she learns to interpret the ways in which different parties perceive reality.

TRANSLATING

The creative follower assists the leader by translating. As a translator of ideas, your role is similar to that of a language translator. You must be able to comprehend an idea and learn how to express that idea using a set of words more readily understood and received by the followers (and the leader). Communication is a two-way process. If the leader is the source of information, the idea is translated from the leader's source language to the target language of the followers. If the followers are the source of information, the reverse process is true when conveying this information to the leader. Even among followers, translation is often necessary. Each department or group inside an organization tends to have a vocabulary that forms its own unique departmental language. I learned that translating ideas from the language of one department to that of another often meant using a different communication method and vocabulary to clarify ideas. This was helpful in getting all parts of the organization traveling in the same direction, guided by the same unifying purpose.

REPACKAGING

Once you understand the message you want to translate, it must be repackaged. Whether a message is simple or complex is not a factor. What matters most is whether the message will be understood by everyone. This is why creative followers must know how to repackage ideas.

The following example is intended to illustrate what I'm suggesting you do as a creative follower to repackage ideas. In this example, the message is coming from the leader through the creative follower to the organization.

In the early days of Chick-fil-A's development of franchise restaurants, the focus was on creating a process for recruiting and selecting Operators and staff members at the home office. We were initially pleased with the results of our recruiting and selection procedures. The process was working well for us, and it seemed easy for us to attract the best of the best.

I knew that, as the organization continued to grow in size, no selection process would permit us to make perfect decisions indefinitely. It stood to reason that the more people we had, the greater our chances for errors. The likelihood that we might end up needing to terminate and replace an Operator or staff employee was increasing. I identified what I thought was a problem and began writing out a plan of action for how we would handle terminations and replacements in the future. When I thought I had it right, I took it to Truett.

I sat down next to his desk to review the plan with him, expecting his approval. Without looking at the document, he said to me, "We won't need that plan; we are not going to be making any changes." To say I was astonished is an understatement.

After I left his office I gave his response a lot of thought. I asked myself several questions. Did he really mean there were never going to be any changes among Operators or employees? Is such an ideal even conceivable? As I continued to rerun the conversation in my mind, though, I had an "aha" moment just when I needed it. Truett was emphasizing to me, his chief follower, his ideal vision for the relationship we would have with our Operators and staff members. In fact, he frequently compared the working relationship to a marriage. Such a comparison is most profound because Truett Cathy believes marriage to be the ideal of a lasting relationship.

What he was telling me in his office that day was not an absolute rule, but it was his way of emphasizing an ideal. He wanted to stress the value he placed on making the right people decisions, and he wanted to communicate that importance to me.

I interpreted a maxim straight from the leader. My next task, as a creative follower, was to translate and repackage this message for the staff. They must understand it, be able to repeat it, and help others to understand it as well. The message from the leader was simple: at Chick-fil-A we will be uncommonly serious about our long-term relationships, and Truett's thoughts on this subject should be understood to be the ideal we must strive to achieve.

The next step was repackaging. Before each final selection interview was completed, I met with the prospective Operator or staff employee, along with the staff member overseeing the selection. I reminded them that our purpose was to find the right people for a long-term relationship. I would say to both of them, "You better be careful in making this decision because you are going to be stuck with each other until one of you either dies or retires." I always smiled just a little when I said that.

From the conversation that day in Truett's office, a brief exchange between the leader and the follower, hundreds of staff employees have learned to know the story well and can explain it to you. It was interpreted, translated, and repackaged so that everyone knew Truett's ideal and goal for the selection process. This repackaged message has grown to become an integral part of the corporate culture. By inserting a touch of humor and a smile, this message has become one of many pieces that convey (or reinforce) Chick-fil-A's unifying purpose in a package everyone can understand, implement, and pass on to others.

REPACKAGING NEGATIVE FEEDBACK

One of the most valuable things you can do for the boss is to gather, interpret, analyze, and translate negative feedback. In order to know how to communicate negative feedback, it is essential for the follower to remember Principle 2: Know Your Boss.

It bears repeating at this point that we must learn everything about the likes and dislikes of the boss. How does the boss like to get information? Should information be in text reports or presented visually, through charts and graphs?

Does it need to be printed, sent electronically, or presented in the form of an oral summary? You must know the preferred format of delivery. Remember, negative or critical feedback is not something you give the boss to solve. When I delivered negative feedback to my boss, I always repackaged it as a problem with at least one possible and practical solution. If I presented multiple solutions, I was prepared to advocate the solution I thought was best. Never punt a problem up the chain of command to your boss. Never present negative feedback in such a manner that it sounds like a personal attack on the boss. The issue is not the boss's intelligence, decision-making skills, or management methods. The issue is a problem in need of immediate attention, and that problem offers an opportunity a creative follower should pursue.

Knowing when to present negative feedback is just as important as knowing how to present it. Followers must consider the mystical element of timing. Timing is critical. Whenever there was distressing news or criticism to deliver, I would test the water to make sure it was the best possible time to talk about it. Timing is critical to the presentation of ideas—positive ones and especially negative ones. Obviously, some things cannot wait. I looked for a window of opportunity to offer some flexibility and I used it.

Negative feedback is not pleasant but it is essential to the growth and advancement of a task or project, and ultimately, for the organization itself. Followers must be able to identify the best possible timing, the appropriate tone, and the most effective approach to use when presenting the leader with negative feedback. Positive feedback feels good, but is it helpful? Positive feedback boosts confidence, but the boost does not last. I'm convinced that positive feedback is of limited benefit. Most of it is less than honest and ranges in value from shallow to deeply insincere. Positive feedback is encouraging and motivational but it does not bring about change. Instead, positive feedback encourages people to do things exactly the way they have in the past; it motivates them to perform at the same level.

Gather, interpret, translate, repackage.

——————— PRINCIPLE 16 ———————
The Only Real
Feedback is Negative

Let me put this another way. Being surrounded by people who agree and get along with every decision has never helped anyone bring change or improvement to any human endeavor. In fact, it is a dangerous environment for the leader. I cannot stress enough the important role the creative follower plays as a source of negative feedback to the boss or leader. Even if you publicize your willingness to listen to negative feedback, you may still not get what you really need. Let's look at feedback and examine the different sources, along with the relative value of different types of feedback.

I cannot emphasize enough the need for reliable negative feedback. Dissent is something that must be encouraged and cultivated. If you think about it, the most useful type of feedback is negative feedback. To be useful, however, feedback must be specific.

Feedback can come in many forms and from many different directions. I will mention three. There is feedback about oneself (from the boss, coworkers, or subordinates); there is feedback within the organization; and there is feedback from outside the organization (from the public or from customers).

The process of becoming more effective as a creative follower starts with seeking feedback about yourself, and you are the one who must cultivate this feedback. Constructive negative feedback is not shallow; it is a catalyst for change in our personal standard operating procedures. Usable negative feedback is specific, including the what, why, and how. I always look forward to receiving authentic negative feedback. It stimulates my commitment to continuous improvement, both personally and professionally.

The only real feedback is negative.

————— PRINCIPLE 17 —————
Cultivate Feedback

At Chick-fil-A, one of my most important communication efforts with the restaurant Operators occurred when I spoke at the annual Operators Seminar. The time and effort I put into that one presentation was huge. It was vitally important for me to do well, but it was even more important, given my commitment to continuous improvement, to know honestly how well I did. I wanted to know specifics: what worked, what did not work. Over time, I found only two staff members who were both capable of and willing to give me not only the positive but also the in-depth and specific negative feedback I was seeking.

When my presentation feedback was "Good speech" or "You did a great job" or "I always look forward to your speech," it didn't tell me anything. What I wanted to know was whether I had been effective in getting my main points across. Did I provoke anyone to think or act differently? Would anyone go home changed or improved by something I said? How many would put the ideas I highlighted into action after they returned home? I had many questions and needed the right type of negative feedback.

To get that kind of feedback, I had to ask the right people for an honest answer. I had to invite complaints, dissent, criticism, and other forms of negative feedback—it had to be an open invitation to share and communicate. Effective leaders develop a culture that welcomes debate and dissent. As a creative follower, you must seek this feedback about yourself and encourage your boss to view negative feedback in the same light. The boss needs negative feedback from your coworkers as well as from you, the creative follower. Everyone has a unique point of view and needs to have a chance to share it with the organization. However, people typically are reluctant to disagree. The politically correct atmosphere in which we live today discourages people from expressing opposing views. Such reluctance often is true in unhealthy workplaces, but it is not true in effective organizations. Followers must understand how to communicate to their leader their thoughts, observations, and feelings.

Ironically, most people will not give much negative feedback to those who can benefit most from hearing it. Instead, coworkers discuss it among themselves in confidential conversations or e-mails. People fear being labeled a complainer by a person who has some say in their career. They are concerned about their future promotions, salary increases, or job performance reviews. An effective leader will constantly reassure those in the organization that bringing negative feedback is a risk-free process.

The creative follower must reach the point where he or she thinks of holding back information in the same way he or she would view holding back inventory or stealing from the company. Think about it this way: if you are receiving a salary, then your point of view and thoughts also belong to the company.

Tight-mouthed workers who do not express their point of view are in a sense "stealing" the intellectual inventory of the organization by not openly sharing. Of course, communication of any type must always be done with courtesy and respect—this is how we package our ideas as professionals.

The boss also needs reliable negative feedback from the customers and clients for whom the company is providing products or services. Organizations use many tools to get customer feedback—cards, surveys, focus groups, and mystery shoppers, to name a few. These tools typically are not cheap. All of these are useful, but I favor the old-fashioned "just talk to the customer" approach. Nevertheless, this face-to-face method should carry a warning label that reads, "This method is ineffective unless properly initiated and executed."

Cultivate feedback.

—————— PRINCIPLE 18 ——————

Ask for Suggestions Rather than Criticism

Face-to-face customer feedback will usually go like this: a well-intentioned manager wanders casually through the dining room, repeating to customers, "How was your meal?"

We have all had something like this happen. There we sit, trying to enjoy a meal and have a conversation, when along comes someone with a name tag, asking a question we are not going to answer honestly unless there was a huge problem with the food or service.

How do you reply? You probably do exactly as I do when I am just trying to enjoy my food and visit with my companions. I say, "Fine." This is what most people do.

Not only is that a waste of time, but also the feedback is misleading. Customers are reluctant to make negative comments because they expect the management to be defensive or confrontational.

At Chick-fil-A, I urged our Operators to talk to customers but to use a different approach. I wanted them to be effective and to invite useable feedback. The question I prefer goes like this: "At Chick-fil-A, we want to constantly improve. What could we do to make your meal more enjoyable?" By asking for suggestions rather than criticism, we put the customers in the position of giving positive feedback rather than negative criticism. For the customer that is a big difference!

No matter what the customers say, moreover, the proper response is to thank them sincerely for the suggestions and to urge them to continue to tell us what improvements they would like see on future visits. This is not the time to defend your business or to try to educate the customer on your procedures and policies. It is not talking time; it is listening time.

Truett Cathy often said, "You don't need to know anything about it to be successful in the restaurant business. Just listen to your customers. They will tell you what to do."

Ask for suggestions rather than criticism.

─────── **PRINCIPLE 19** ───────

Always Apologize, Never Explain

Customer complaints are an excellent source of feedback. Because customers pay for what they receive, they have a keen interest in registering complaints—but only when the service or product has been very disappointing. For every customer who brings a verbal complaint, there could be dozens more unhappy customers who never said a word but simply walked away displeased about their experience. These same people are likely to deliver their feedback about the experience to someone else in the future, and it will not be complimentary. After a customer walks out the door, there is no way to turn a negative experience into an opportunity to apologize or to create an emotional connection by doing something positive and memorable.

Therefore, a customer complaint represents a colossal opportunity. It is a shame that the opportunity usually turns into a dismal disappointment for both parties, because it does not have to be that way. Customer complaints can end with the customer walking away with a more favorable impression of the organization as a result of what was done to correct the problem, and the organization can learn lessons that may prevent the same thing from happening in the future.

There is a right way and a wrong way to deal with complaints. First, when dealing with customer complaints, I always apologize, never explain. I find that the following procedure seems to work best: I apologize, whether the problem is my fault or not—I have a no-fault apology policy. I deliver the apology as if I am the only one responsible. I take responsibility, and even if the customer is wrong, mistaken, or unreasonable, I treat the customer as if he or she is right and reasonable.

Second, I make it a point never to explain anything. Do not give details about why something happened this way or that way. This is a good policy whether you are dealing with customers or approaching the boss about some business matter. I do not give reasons, because the customer doesn't want to hear it. As soon as you start to explain, the customer perceives your reasons to be an attempt to defend yourself, your fellow workers, your boss, or your company. It appears to the complainant that you are avoiding responsibility for what has happened and that you are making the customer out to be the offender, the one who has disturbed the peace. Rather than offering up a defense, therefore, I ask the customer to explain how the situation looked and felt, and then I ask for suggestions on how to avoid repeating this situation in the future.

Next, I turn the tables on the customer and put them in charge by asking what would constitute a suitable response for this unfortunate situation. I ask, "What would you like me to do?" After the customer makes a suggestion, I try to exceed expectations and do more than what was asked. Again, this is just good practice. When dealing with critical feedback, apologize, fix the problem, and exceed expectations in some way.

In the Shadow of Greatness

Leave a positive impression and learn from the criticism, because all negative feedback is beneficial in some manner.

I also have found that, like customers, the boss usually does not want an explanation. Even when the boss asks for an explanation, that is not what she wants. An explanation sounds defensive and evasive, neither of which the boss wants to hear. So take responsibility, apologize, and fix the situation the way the boss likes it done.

Perhaps you do not work in a retail situation, with the public, or with customers. You do, however, have a boss. And if you do work for a boss, the boss is your customer! These principles work equally well with those in authority.

Always apologize, never explain.

PRINCIPLE 20
Confront Grumbling and Murmuring

Although useful and responsive feedback from well-informed critics and highly motivated individuals is priceless, there also is a nonconstructive type of dissent. I do not call it feedback because it seldom travels back to the source of the action that provoked the dissent. This form of dissent does not move up; instead, it tends to spread down and out. A creative follower knows the difference between constructive and nonconstructive dissent.

I cannot imagine a boss who would ever tolerate grumbling and murmuring. I know I did not have patience for these things. The negativity generated by grumbling and murmuring is poison to the morale of those in the organization and costs a great deal of productive time and energy. It always troubles me when an individual or group is so unhappy that they attempt to disrupt things or make someone else look bad. The creative follower's task is to make the boss look good; seek to understand the nature of the things that potentially make the boss look bad and address these first.

GRUMBLING

I don't know why people conclude that it is profitable for them to cause trouble. Does it really make them feel better? Do they think it raises their esteem among their peers? If so, they are wrong. In fact, it has the opposite effect, lowering opinions about their attitude and actions on the job.

That kind of thinking is simply beyond my ability to understand. All of us have seen it happen and know how destructive it can be. This kind of behavior not only is disruptive to the group's effort but also is most destructive to the reputation of the one causing the disruption. At some point, the person doing the grumbling is going to be a big loser.

While serving on many governing boards and committees over the years, I sat through many meetings. One evening there was a board meeting for a children's home. A new program was introduced and widely supported. Almost everyone seemed to feel good about the idea. There was a unanimous vote to proceed. After the meeting, however, someone said to me, "I voted for it, but I didn't like it and don't think we should be doing this." He went on to tell me all the things he did not like about the program, and he kept saying, "I started to say . . ."

But he had said nothing. This is exactly the kind of grumbling I dislike—declining to speak before a decision, and then saying negative things after the decision has been made.

When I encounter this, I always confront the person and ask why she or he did not bring these things up for consideration in the meeting, to see whether other people thought the same way. It is a serious mistake to harbor these kinds of thoughts after a decision is made. It undermines the whole process used to make the decision in the first place.

Unfortunately, this illustrates something I saw many times in business, on governing boards, and in committees of all types of organizations. Thus, I made a conscious decision never to be an after-the-meeting grumbler. If you are a follower dedicated to the unifying purpose, there is no point in sitting back and remaining silent. Open expression of multiple points of view and vigorous discussion leads to unification of effort.

The importance of expressing one's point of view cannot be overemphasized. It was a policy I followed whenever I chaired a meeting or had any opportunity to stimulate honest and open discussion. This is the best way to discourage after-meeting grumbling.

MURMURING

If you allow murmuring to thrive, it will be very destructive to any organization. Murmurers tend to deliver dissent to people who can do nothing about it, and some seem to go for quantity rather than quality when it comes to complaining. Instead of properly addressing concerns to an individual who may hear, understand, and possibly change the direction of a situation, they choose to tell people who can do nothing other than listen and repeat. This unhealthy murmuring can easily spread through an organization, like a contagious disease. Murmuring is something most bosses do not have time to deal with, and it is something followers can monitor and address before a little office talk becomes a serious issue. In my role as a follower, I always worked to eliminate murmuring.

When people are encouraged to speak up and they can see what happens when others speak up—that there are no negative results—murmuring loses favor. An effective leader knows this and tries to build an environment of open communication. The creative follower can assist and support that open environment by example and by keeping in touch with what is going on. As a follower, if I heard people murmuring, I confronted them and urged them to tell someone who could actually do something about it.

Confront grumbling and murmuring.

———— **PRINCIPLE 21** ————
Encourage Your Boss

By now, it should be clear that the creative follower plays many roles you probably were not expecting. Removing obstacles along the way, such as murmuring and other nonconstructive criticism, is just one role. Another role relates to encouragement. We typically hear about encouragement coming down the chain of command, but we seldom think about how beneficial it is moving up the organizational chart.

Nonetheless, encouragement can and should move up the chain of command. The boss or the leader needs to be encouraged—as Truett used to say, "Do you know how to tell if someone needs encouragement? He is breathing!" Real encouragement delivered with sincerity does not look or feel as if one is trying to win personal favor, though it does take skill and finesse, and timing is critically important.

My primary care physician of many years, Byron F. Harper, Jr., was a very effective encourager. I still have the notes of encouragement he wrote to me. One day he said to me, "Do you know who needs the most encouragement but gets the least? The boss. Most people do not think the boss needs encouragement, but believe me, he does."

That conversation often comes to mind, and I realize he was right. President Harry S Truman had a sign on his desk that read, "The buck stops here." For many important decisions, the boss dwells in a lonely place—at the top of the decision-making/problem-solving chain. Think of the times you have been at the end of the decision chain and have experienced that loneliness. Do you sometimes second-guess yourself the day after a big decision, even wondering whether you made the right choice? Did you have all the facts? Did you spend too much? Did you get good advice beforehand? Should you change that direction? Like you, I have those thoughts and I need confirmation that I made a good decision. If it looks like things are not working out, I need to know what corrective action to take.

More importantly, if I felt that way about my decisions in my circle of authority, surely my boss felt that way too. Did Truett need encouragement? Probably! That is when I decided to become my boss's encourager.

Truett did not like to read detailed written reports. He liked brief oral summaries. He did not like to hear about problems, but he appreciated it when they were handled promptly and efficiently. With that in mind, I formulated my encouragement plan for my boss.

Every day that we both were in town at the same time, I went into his office to encourage him. I presented brief oral summaries as status updates. I wanted him to know that we were on track to accomplish our objectives and that he and our executive committee had made good decisions. I also would tell him about any corrective actions that were being taken for things not on track. I wanted to reassure him.

Keep your boss informed. Any boss will appreciate this

kind of information. But never bring problems without some type of recommended solution.

One by-product of my encouragement was that Truett felt comfortable leaving more and more of the responsibility of managing Chick-fil-A to me. This confidence in me increased for many reasons. First, I never sugarcoated bad news or exaggerated good news. Second, whenever I explained difficulties we had encountered, I always matched it with the corrective action we were already taking. Third, I never used these sessions to call attention to my own performance. Fourth, he knew he could trust me because of my absolute loyalty to him and our corporate purpose.

I know my form of encouragement was meaningful to him, because on several visits to his office after I retired, he said, "Nobody keeps me informed the way you did."

For any encouragement to be effective, it must be specific, sincere, real, and truthful. Encouragement of the boss is no different.

Encourage your boss.

CHAPTER 9

Taking Responsibility

The foundational force of the art of Creative Followership is taking responsibility. When I was a teenager working at Roy Hancock's neighborhood grocery store, I learned a great deal about taking responsibility. Mr. Hancock was a good boss, teacher, coach, and encourager. He was a former World War II army officer who had worked in A&P supermarkets before the war. When he returned to the States, he opened his own neighborhood grocery store, where I worked for two years, starting at age 15. In that store, I learned many character-building life lessons that had a tremendous impact on me, particularly in the area of customer service and quality. (A note to those readers who are still in their teens: What you learn at your first jobs—the jobs that likely pay minimum wage—should be valued over and above the financial compensation you actually receive for your time. You may be working for minimum wage now, but the real-life lessons learned will be priceless in your future.)

One thing that impressed me about Roy Hancock was the way he connected with his customers. He had to have an edge to compete with the national grocery store chains that were not far away. Mr. Hancock's edge was his personalized customer service and friendliness. He put a great deal of effort into interacting with his customers. But he was not like the greeter at the door who says, "Welcome to Walmart!" He was genuine. He knew or knew something about everyone who entered the store. Mr. Hancock could pick up a conversation from the previous time he had seen a customer. Even now, sixty years later, I can still picture him standing there with his Zippo lighter in one hand, tapping his unfiltered cigarette against the lighter to pack the tobacco down, all the while carrying on conversations about this and that with the customers.

Mr. Hancock went fishing on Wednesday afternoons and took short vacations during the summer. Even though I was very young, he would leave me in charge of the store when he was away. One time, the Luzianne representative visited the store while Mr. Hancock was away on vacation. Although the store sold the popular Luzianne brand of coffee, we did not carry Luzianne tea. The representative pointed out how

Roy Hancock and his daughter Carole

well the Luzianne coffee sold in the store and what a smart decision it would be for me to take the initiative and sell Luzianne tea as well. He convinced me that it was the very best tea—and not only that, but for a short time he could offer a special deal to entice us to start selling Luzianne tea.

How could I say no to such a convincing presentation? I was excited about this business opportunity, so I told him to send us some tea as well as the usual coffee order. Certain that a home run was possible with this, I took the risk and initiative and signed the purchase order.

Something I failed to consider, however, was that a small grocery store is limited in the amount and variety of inventory it can carry. A little neighborhood store cannot just stock up on every item that might sell. In addition, tea and coffee, like many other grocery items, have a shelf life. They must sell quickly or they will get stale and go to waste. When I told Mr. Hancock what I had done, he was not excited about stocking another brand of tea. He was very direct and to the point with me. I recall him standing there, tapping down his cigarette in a slightly different manner than he did with customers. Mr. Hancock smoked when the store was busy with customers, he smoked when it was empty, and he smoked in the many times in between. I guess you could say this was one of those in-between times.

I learned in very specific terms how a business like this grocery store—his grocery store—had a purpose. The purpose of this store was to make money. He said he must make a profit; this profit was how he made his living and how he paid my salary. A store earns no profit from unsold merchandise; instead, unsold merchandise reduces the profit margin.

Mr. Hancock spoke clearly and I clearly understood what he was saying. Plus, I already understood Followership Principle 7: Take Responsibility. Therefore, my goal and purpose in life was now one thing and one thing only: I would sell every one of those boxes of tea, and failure was not an option. Because I had placed the order, it was my job to take responsibility and to see to it that the store made a profit from my decision.

Make Your Decisions Good

In that moment I had a flash of sudden awareness—I learned what it means to own a decision, to take responsibility for my actions, and to make or turn my decision into a good one. I made the decision, I would own it, I was responsible for it, and I was going to make it right!

Regardless of your position in an organization or your level of commitment to Creative Followership, everyone has to make decisions. People ask me all the time, "How do you make good decisions?" I have heard many people say you learn to make good decisions by making bad ones. Originally, I thought that answer to be not all that helpful, until I took the time to carefully think about what happens when a person makes a bad decision. In thinking about decision making, I have learned that the issue is not about making good decisions. The real issue is making your decisions good.

This is exactly what I chose to do with my decision to order that tea. To start, I bought the first box of Luzianne tea to be sure it really was the best. That way, I could tell customers it was what we used at my home. Next, I prepared my sales pitch and went to work selling.

The good news is that I was successful. I took responsibility and made it right. A creative follower must be committed to personal responsibility. In fact, before very long, Luzianne tea was flying out the door with the shoppers at

Triangle Grocery. We sold more Luzianne than the other two brands of tea combined. And I was then—and still am—sold on Luzianne tea. If you open the cabinet at my house today, you will see a shelf stocked with Luzianne tea.

On the other hand, if the tea had failed to move quickly from the shelves, things would have been different. I made my decision the right decision by taking responsibility for making customers aware of this excellent new product, and I sold them on the idea. Workers, followers, bosses, and even leaders should spend less time deliberating good decisions and concentrate more on making their decisions good.

NO PERFECT DECISIONS

There is no such thing as a perfect decision. You know this even though you may not have given it much thought. Think about it now. If, following a decision, everything in the world were to stand still and not change for however many days it took for that decision to be fully complete and all the results to be known, you could possibly say, "I have made a good decision." But we live in a dynamic world of change and motion, a place where nothing ever stays perfectly still. Think about how many unknown factors and people are likely to weigh in on your decision (including people who help you carry out your decision).

By the time you begin the execution of your well-thought-out plan, the original conditions have probably changed significantly. Decision making is most often (but not always) a process of making corrections and adjustments to the original plan to make it a success. Implementation requires many modifications. The plan you decided on at the outset and what you ended up doing during execution may not resemble each other. So, what did you gain by taking so long to make that perfect decision?

It is not so much a matter of following a certain process to be sure you are making a good decision; rather, it is a matter of making your decision good. Good decision makers work this way, and that is why people look up to them. People on the outside of the process may miss this fact. They see only the finished product resulting from the initial decision and not the many modifications and changes that came along the way, as the idea (decision) came into existence. Can you remember a single decision that worked out exactly as you first expected? I can't!

THERE ARE NO FORMULAS

If you think about it, whenever we make decisions we are thinking about things that are going to happen in the future. Some decisions are about what is going to happen in the next fifteen seconds, but most decisions concern what is going to happen much further in the future.

I have read many books and sat through seminars about decision making. I vividly recall one presentation about how to make good decisions. All sorts of diagrams, featuring everything from complex matrix systems to simple two-column pro-and-con lists were presented, supposedly providing detail about how to weigh this side and that side of an equation. The decision-making process was dissected and examined. But there was no way I was going to be able to use that type of system. To my mind, all of the many different processes and systems designed to help a person make good decisions have something in common—I could never make a decision using any of them! These processes do not fit my personality.

I realize that everyone is different, and some people may be able to use these devices. Some people like to go off into a corner, take out a pen and paper, and start drawing columns, weighing pros and cons. I suppose some use a mathematical equation to reach a conclusion about the best decision to make. Everyone should decide for himself or herself what works.

Personally, when I am dealing with a decision that affects a lot of people, I like to get the issue out in an open discussion with several people. My favorite method is to put together a group of stakeholders and wise counsel to think through the details and argue different options. I have found this is very helpful. It helps me to think my position through and balance it alongside other positions. When other people tell me what they think about an issue, it forces me to look at both sides of the issue. The options then include either agreeing with them or changing their mind. Following that process, I move forward knowing where and why I stand on the issues. The exercise creates awareness about important aspects of the decision that I should be considering. For me, this is a much better procedure, and it is an indispensable process for my decision making.

BE FLEXIBLE

My working relationship with Truett depended not just on my ability to make good decisions but also on making those decisions good. This is something that would not have been possible had I not invested time in learning what was important to Truett. He understood that I would look out for him and work for his best interests. As his follower, I had to be able to predict his response, and he knew that he could count on me to use my best judgment in the process. But I did not necessarily do things exactly the way he would have done them. He got the results he wanted but not always as he would have done it, and that was all right. We agreed on *what* was to be done, but we both had to be flexible on *how* it was to be done. That works when there is two-way loyalty and trust between the leader and the follower. Truett had complete trust in me because of my absolute loyalty to him.

Even the best-laid plans have to be modified. Some decisions are point-blank and have immediate consequences. But most business decisions are measured by delayed or long-term results. It is the small but creative adjustments made along the way that make the difference between success and failure.

Here is what I have concluded about decision making: you have to take responsibility for making a decision good by constantly nurturing it, guiding it, and reevaluating the intermediate results to see whether it is taking you where you wanted to go. Circumstances are always changing; unforeseen obstacles, opportunities, and adversities just happen. Don't give up, don't give in, and be flexible in the execution to fit the situation. It is up to you, and it is an active process.

Make your decisions good.

—————— PRINCIPLE 23 ——————
Be Assertive

Creative followers are not passive individuals who are afraid to make a move without the boss's approval. As I said before, the best kind of followers are mustangs. Mustangs are assertive. To get the right result, I was assertive in my efforts to move that tea. That is what it takes to be successful in nearly any venture in life. To do something that makes a difference, you have to push yourself, challenge yourself, and sometimes put yourself out beyond the comfort zone. This is what makes a follower valuable to the boss. Make yourself valuable; be assertive!

Assertiveness is nothing more than openly expressing yourself in a manner that gets things done but does not hurt other people. At times, it means saying yes and moving into the unknown. Other times it means having the courage to say no to protect your rights as well as the rights of others. It does not mean that you dominate others. In fact, when handled carefully, it makes others feel that they are valuable and worthwhile. It will make others see that you are working in their best interest and not just in your own.

It matters little how it makes you feel; do not let your feelings get in the way. It may seem awkward or uncomfortable, but in the end you will be glad you pushed yourself to do something rather than sitting on the sidelines doing nothing. Sometimes you have to assume a role, much like an actor, to get a task completed well. At Mr. Hancock's store I played the role of an enthusiastic tea salesman.

I have cast myself in many different roles, but when I take on a new role I make sure I know what I am doing, that I want to play this role, and that I can do it with confident assertiveness. There is a saying in the theater: "Don't get caught acting." Do not try to play a role unless you can be genuinely enthusiastic about it. You must literally live the role, and it might cost a huge price if you cast yourself in a role you do not believe you can fill. Everybody quickly spots a fake. Be authentic!

On the other hand, people who lack assertiveness live a life with less contentment and peace. People who choose not to be assertive find themselves pushed into corners. They will agree to do things that are inconvenient or that they do not really want to do. They cannot seem to say no to others without feeling guilty. To avert the guilt, they say nothing at all or they reluctantly—and dishonestly—say yes. As a result, they build up resentment toward others. Sometimes this leads to aggression at inappropriate times or toward people who have not done anything wrong. In addition, it directly affects one's confidence, which produces a loss of internal fortitude to be assertive in the future—it is a vicious spiral down.

Be assertive.

PRINCIPLE 24

Learn to Say No

The word no might be the most important word in the English language. Proper use of this word will signal to the world around you who you really are. It indicates what you really believe, what you stand for, the value you place on your integrity, and the limit of your courage. When it is properly used, you do not have to write it in bold letters or italics or underline it. When you say it in a conversation, you do not have to shout it aggressively or feel like you need a bullhorn to announce it. Just a soft, firm no will work just fine, if it is sincerely and assertively stated.

This two-letter word can be the most useful in a creative follower's toolbox of words. It can prevent you from losing your integrity. Saying no can keep you from deviating from the unifying purpose. You can protect your boss from embarrassment. It can secure your role as a valuable follower. There are people who have a gift for making people say yes rather than no—and a creative follower must be on guard when in the presence of those who make it hard to say no.

When you are negotiating to buy or sell an automobile, a horse, or real estate, if you are not willing or not able to say no, you will never make the best possible deal—and you could get stuck with a really bad one. If the wrong person proposed marriage to you, would you say no? Of course, you would! But what would you do if the boss asked you to tell a lie? Would you be able to say no in the very same way? You can and you should be able to say it quickly and assertively in both cases.

While I was working as a restaurant equipment salesman, I negotiated a cost-plus contract to furnish all the equipment for a new restaurant. The buyer was a good-natured, easygoing man whom my boss perceived to be very trusting and naive. The boss told me not to let the buyer know the full extent of the discounts we received from the manufacturers, because the buyer should not know our real cost.

This was my reply: "I will not lie to you and I will not lie for you." The subject was never brought up again.

Learning how and when to say no is essential for confident assertiveness and responsible decision making.

Learn to say no.

CHAPTER 10

Exceeding Expectations

PRINCIPLE 25
Do it Right

The creative follower will do what the boss does not like to do or does not do well. I have presented these principles in previous chapters, but I bring them up again to emphasize how to apply them. A wise follower will make certain that what he or she does for the boss is done right! There is no advantage in doing something poorly for the boss. Your reputation for doing things well and responsibly lives or dies according to the quality of your work.

I expect and demand from myself a superior performance; therefore, anyone who does something for me should expect to perform at the level I require of myself. As a child, I learned from my father to strive for work with zero defects. He had been a farmer, so even after we moved to the city, he planted a large backyard garden. (During World War II, we called them victory gardens.) My brothers and I cared for the garden. I hated the job, especially the weeding. One reason was that Daddy expected perfection. If I did not remove every weed, he would say, "Any job worth doing is worth doing right" and send me back to do it over. I hated the weeds. I hated the garden. I hated the discipline. It took time for me to appreciate the valuable lesson he taught me. Later, I would treasure the lesson and the memory of him saying, "Any job worth doing is worth doing right."

Do it right.

—————— PRINCIPLE 26 ——————
Do More than is Expected

Something else has always driven me internally. Making decisions and then taking responsibility for them has to do with things that we have done already. If I say I am going to take responsibility for a decision I made, I am looking back to a point in space and time where I made that decision. There is an expectation that, to take responsibility, I must fulfill the obligations of that decision. However, fulfilling the obligation or meeting the expectation is never enough. I have to do more than is expected.

You will not go far doing only what is expected.

I just am not happy unless I have exceeded what is expected of me. To be successful as a creative follower, you will need this kind of internal drive. If you do not already have it, try stimulating it by giving it a shot. Go ahead—exceed expectations, and do it on purpose. Do not just do what you have to do to get by. Instead, plan it out and exceed what you know is going to be the requirement for a task or project. I guarantee that at the end of the day, you will have a sense of accomplishment that far exceeds the feeling one gets from a job well done. The added sense of accomplishment is so exhilarating that to me it is addictive. The behavior of going above and beyond makes me feel so good that I have to repeat it.

Do more than is expected.

——————— **PRINCIPLE 27** ———————

Do Not Wait to Be Told What to Do

Creative followers do not sit around waiting for their next assignment; they create assignments on their own. Great leaders are great because they have surrounded themselves with followers who not only get things done, and get them done with excellence, but also find things that need to be done and accomplish them before they are asked to do so.

Performing to the best of one's ability in the eyes of the boss is easy—just plan to always exceed the boss's expectations. You can do more—go ahead and go the extra mile. Do not wait for the boss to tell you to do something; anticipate it and do it before the request comes. Determine the need that must be met, the problem that must be solved, and take responsibility for it before it becomes an issue. Most importantly, do it better than it has ever been done before. Figure out what you need to do, and do it ahead of time.

Consider what extra touches your boss would like and then add those to the job or project. Always shoot for doing more than is expected, as the boss likes it done, and ahead of schedule. You will soon be recognized as the one who never fails to deliver. What kind of boss or leader would not want someone like you on his or her team?

I have seen these principles at work many times, but a few instances stand out in my memory. During my lifetime, for example, I calculate that I have eaten more than 82,000 meals, but there are very few times I remember receiving service that went above and beyond all expectations. Out of 82,000, I will never forget one meal.

A few years ago, while I was traveling in Pennsylvania, my wife and I stopped for lunch at a family-owned restaurant. We had the pleasure of being served by a truly excellent waitress—let's call her Cindy. She immediately recognized that we had never been there before and set about making us feel at home. She told us about their fabulous food, including bread, pies, and pastry baked on the premises. Her attention to detail exceeded our expectations. She anticipated our every desire. The food was perfect and the service was outstanding. Even though we were older than Cindy, she insisted on referring to us as "you kids." When she handed us our check, she invited us to return, and she gave us a hug and a kiss on the cheek! That meal is what I call a memorable experience. Cindy did more than we expected; she did not wait to be told what to do. I wish Cindy could serve us lunch again tomorrow. Would you like to join us?

I am certain Cindy's boss did not tell her to give us a hug and a kiss on the cheek. She took responsibility, did not wait to be told what to do, did more than was expected, and created a wonderfully memorable customer experience.

WHEN THE BOSS IS NOT LOOKING

Sometimes we do things at work when no one is looking. The question is whether we will perform at the same level as we do when people are looking. Creative followers will do just that—exceed expectations even when no one is looking, even when there is a chance no one will know or understand what effort went into a task or project.

What really counts is doing things the right way, the same way, even when no one is looking. I cannot stress enough how important to your career and future advancement this principle is. You can avoid so many pitfalls if you practice this one extremely simple rule of thumb. For instance, apply it and you will escape the dilemma of having to be on alert to change the level of your performance when the boss is looking—it won't matter, because you just perform and behave at your best all of the time. If the boss comes up from behind and you are not expecting to see him or her, things will always be up to par and as they should be. Most importantly, you will know you did your best at all times, and that carries its own reward. How can you be honest with yourself and do less?

When I was a youngster working a part-time job, I remember hearing fellow employees say, "When the boss is away is when we play." Years ago, a youngster named Norm "Red" Witten didn't buy that kind of misdirection. His boss, Jim Ball, Operator of the Chick-fil-A restaurant in Newmarket North Mall in Newport News, Virginia, said of Red, "When I want to have my restaurant really cleaned and put in best order, I take a few days off and leave a teenager named Norm 'Red' Witten in charge."

You see, rather than seeing an opportunity to play, Red took responsibility. He did not wait for his boss to tell him what to do. When the boss was away, he took advantage of the opportunity, worked at his highest level, and motivated the other employees to do the same. He performed even better when the boss was away! His performance was recognized and rewarded many times over the years that followed.

Truett Cathy, Lynn and Red Witten

Soon, Red, at the age of 19, became the Operator of his own Chick-fil-A restaurant, in Tower Mall in Portsmouth, Virginia. He took a restaurant that had been open for twenty-three months but had never made a profit and made it profitable from the first month. Within Chick-fil-A, his success is legendary! Red has earned Chick-fil-A's highest sales performance award by reaching his Symbol of Success goal five times!

What is most compelling here—and this is what really counts—is that the boss will know what you are truly made of by measuring how well you perform when no one is looking. Not only will the boss know, but also your coworkers will know, your customers will know—everyone will know!

Do not wait to be told what to do.

─────── PRINCIPLE 28 ───────
Do the Dirty and Difficult Jobs

Do you want to go one step further in exceeding expectations? You can, if you consider the issue of how one handles the unpleasant, the mundane, and even the dirty. Will you honestly give these the same attention as the high-profile and pleasant tasks?

Do you like doing the dirty jobs? Most people avoid them or try to work themselves out of dirty-job status soon. It is just human nature; we want to avoid what is painful and unpleasant. Therefore, your boss is going to notice all the dirty jobs you are doing, and doing successfully, without any reminders or complaints. Doing so really gets the boss's attention! An employee who honestly respects the boss, the job, and the brand is valuable to the business, but an employee who gets done the things that no one else wants to do really stands out.

I would like to persuade you to become that follower. Take on the most difficult or the dirtiest job you can find, and then be sure that you do the best job ever done with it. The sense of personal victory from conquering your worst fear is its own reward, but the dividends also may extend beyond this one event. This is a living and dynamic process. As your personal stock begins to rise, you may find yourself elevated to jobs and tasks that are far from what most would consider the difficult and dirty jobs. You also will find that you respond more easily to all tasks, whether they are the most difficult and the dirtiest or the easiest and cleanest in the business, and as a result your overall performance is going to be noticed. In fact, you will find yourself doing the most difficult jobs in the organization and receiving appropriate recognition for your performance. You can and must go above and beyond in a wide variety of tasks, without regard for how unpleasant or challenging these tasks may be, if you want the ultimate in personal satisfaction.

Do the dirty and difficult jobs.

—————— PRINCIPLE 29 ——————
Take Risks

As you continue to grow and become more confident in exceeding expectations, do not rule out pushing the envelope. I have already emphasized how much I would rather rein in mustangs than push mules. The mustangs are the ones that stand out. You cannot stand out from the crowd and be the most valuable follower if you do not take a step forward. Do not be timid. Timidity can rob you of your opportunities for personal growth. If you see something that needs someone to work on it, and you believe you have the best solution to a problem, then go ahead. Do it. Get it done. I want to be the person who makes things happen. Who do you want to be?

To achieve personal and professional growth, we all need the opportunity to fail. We do not necessarily need to fail, but we need that risk factor present in order to make success meaningful. If you are not out on the edge—and occasionally over the edge—of your authority, you are unlikely to ever accomplish anything beyond the routine. You do not need to fail in order to grow, but failure could be a good experience that will stimulate growth and future success.

And even if you do fail, what is the worst thing that can happen? Although it was painful to face the consequences of my failures, I never stood before a firing squad! In fact, I have never been fired from a job.

You have probably heard the old saying that it is easier to get forgiveness than permission. This holds especially true for creative followers when it comes to taking risks. There are no advancements without risk. Risk carries the probability of failure, and everyone naturally has a fear of failure. But we cannot grow unless we learn. I found that I learned much more from my failed efforts than I did from those things that were both effortless and successful.

Would you like to be a follower who demonstrates superior performance with extraordinary results? Then you must take some risks. What should you do if something goes wrong? It's simple: if you fail, own it, fix it, and tell the boss quickly.

Take risks.

—————— **PRINCIPLE 30** ——————
Bad News Does Not Improve with Age

Keep this in mind if you fail: General Creighton Abrams said, "Bad news does not improve with age." The sooner you can report what has happened, the sooner you can assist in finding a resolution and the better the outcome will be. I have always liked to clean up my spills before someone stepped in them. You can correct most failures if you take corrective action at once, but you never want to appear to be concealing or covering up something that needed to be corrected, especially if the bad news is a result of something for which you are responsible. Delay can cause a little incident to explode into a catastrophe.

Given the choice of over- or undercorrection, I always chose to do more than the minimum and to do it promptly. Therefore, move quickly, take action, and never delay telling your boss the bad news. But, with that bad news, have your solution already under way.

Bad news does not improve with age.

CHAPTER 11

Develop Yourself

I f you have absorbed and applied the principles already discussed, congratulations! You are well on your way to a much more successful and satisfying career. However, Creative Followership does not end with what we have discussed up to this point. There is more. If you have been practicing these principles for a while, it is highly likely that you have expanded your horizons, broadened your borders, been noticed, and assumed more responsibility and authority than you had previously enjoyed.

With the added responsibility of being a creative follower comes certain principles for expanded areas of responsibility. Your expanded role as a creative follower is likely to be in a different position in the organization—or soon will be. It is time to think of yourself in a different light than you may have previously, especially if you were an entry-level worker at the beginning of the process. It is time you began to think of yourself not as just a worker or an employee but as an executive. Assume the role; it is yours for the taking.

Assuming you have (or will have in the near future) an effective leader to work with, you probably have noticed a few things about him or her that you might not have been expecting. For instance, effective leaders usually do not give highly detailed instructions; it is up to you, the creative follower, to interpret and expand into executable form the goals, objectives, and big-picture tasks of the unifying purpose. To become successful at putting everything together will require you to exercise discipline in the area of self-development. The following four principles related to self-development go hand in hand with Creative Followership.

———— **PRINCIPLE 31** ————
Do Not Be
Easily Discouraged

For most people, dealing with personal discouragement is tough. Discouragement can drag you down quickly unless you learn to deal with it in a positive manner.

At a young age, I realized that everyone I know faces

some form of discouragement in life. I also noticed that a person could control how discouragement affected his or her life. By the time I reached high school, I had decided that in the face of discouragement I would remind myself, "I am not easily discouraged." It was amazing how that helped me through difficult times.

Overcoming discouragement is a favorite topic when I speak to young people, and I like to tell them this story: When I was a teenager, during the fabulous fifties, my friends and I visited drive-in restaurants several evenings during the week. This really was a popular thing to do; it was much like a scene from the movies *American Graffiti* and *Grease*.

A friend of mine was dating a girl from Brown High School, a school not far from ours. We frequently spotted a gray Buick full of girls from Brown at a drive-in called Uncle Tom's. My friend's girlfriend and her sister, Oleta McKibben, were usually in that car. Oleta was the prettiest of those Brown High girls! She was spunky and I liked her.

Immediately, however, I faced discouragement. Oleta did not like me! Even though I tried my best to turn on the charm and my most likable personality, nothing seemed to work with her. She was not impressed.

I wanted Oleta to go out with me, but I suspected she might turn me down. I did not want to face outright rejection, so I asked a friend of hers to check and see whether Oleta would say yes if I asked her out. Her friend came back with, "She is not interested."

I really liked Oleta and did not want to give up, so I asked a friend who was dating Oleta's sister to see if he could arrange a double date with Oleta and me. Again, word came back, "She is not interested."

Then I learned that she was having a birthday party. I was certain I could find a way to get invited. I asked her sister to get me an invitation. Just like before, the word was "She is not interested."

Well, I am not easily discouraged. So I went anyway! The next weekend, on June 6, 1954, we had our first date. After that day, I never dated another girl. For more than fifty years, Oleta has been the most important person in my life, my most trusted adviser, my greatest encourager, and my wife.

I have often thought how different my life would have been if I had become discouraged, had given up, and had not gone uninvited to that birthday party. I think of how much I would have missed, how much less fulfilling my life would have been!

It would be impossible to count how many times I have reminded myself, "I am not easily discouraged." Hundreds—maybe thousands. This reminder, which has become Creative Followership Principle 31: Do Not Be Easily Discouraged, has affected my life positively more times than I can count. There are occasions when I use it several times during the week. It is my choice; I will not be easily discouraged.

Another example of how important it is not to be easily discouraged happened in 1971, as we were working to expand

Oleta McKibben and Jimmy Collins, 1954

Chick-fil-A. By the end of 1970, we had seven Chick-fil-A restaurants in shopping malls—three in Georgia, two in North Carolina, one in South Carolina, and one in Texas. Not many for three years of effort.

Even though enclosed malls were opening at an increasing rate all over the country, we were having great difficulty getting locations. The malls wanted tearooms, coffee shops, and fine dining. In addition, most of the major mall developers wanted only tenants with AAA credit ratings, which Chick-fil-A did not have. Chick-fil-A offered high-volume, quick service, but the response was, "We are not interested." I had heard that before, many times, but I am not easily discouraged.

When we learned that the Rouse Company, one of the premier mall developers, was to open a new mall in Atlanta in the summer of 1971, we went after a location. Off I went to their offices in Maryland, armed with determination and enthusiasm. Unfortunately, they did not want what they thought of as a fried chicken restaurant in one of their classy malls. I made so many trips to their office that when I arrived the receptionist would announce, "Chicken Little is here again." They were courteous but firm in their reply: "We are not interested." But I am not easily discouraged.

Then, when we learned that the leasing agents were visiting the construction site, Truett and I took Chick-fil-A food to them. Still they said, "We are not interested."

That is when I started a postcard deluge. We had picture postcards of Chick-fil-A sandwiches and the Oglethorpe Mall restaurant in Savannah. Each day, every day, I sent a postcard to the vice president of leasing. Typical messages were "Only Chick-fil-A serves America's favorite main dish as a sand-wich!" "At Chick-fil-A in Greenbriar Mall, 1970, sales equal $626.32 per square foot, without opening on Sunday!" "At Chick-fil-A, service IS instantaneous!" "At Chick-fil-A, we have no bones to sell, only chicken!"

11-24-70

OF OGLETHORPE MALL
7604 Abercorn Ext.
Savannah, Ga. 31406
Chick-fil-a Inc., Hapeville, Ga. 30354, establishing
company _____ quick service food units
such as this in regional type shopping centers.

IF YOU HAD A FAST FOOD
OPERATION THAT LOOKED
LIKE THIS IN PERIMETER
MALL, WOULD YOU HAVE
TO APOLOGIZE FOR IT'S
APPEARANCE?

JIM COLLINS

52324-C

dp DEXTER PRESS, INC.

Post Card

5¢ U.S. POSTAGE

MR. ROBERT D. RIEDY
THE ROUSE COMPANY
COLUMBIA, MARYLAND
21043

2-26-71

DEAR MR. WOLF:

CHICK-FIL-A OF GREENBRIAR
ATLANTA, GA. PAID
$36.03 PER SQ. FT.
RENT DURING 1970!

JIM COLLINS

MR. LARRY WOLF
THE ROUSE COMPANY
COLUMBIA, MD.
21043

3-15-71

OF OGLETHORPE MALL
7604 Abercorn Ext.
Savannah, Ga. 31406
Chick-fil-a Inc., Hapeville, Ga. 30354, establishing
company _____ quick service food units
such as this in regional type shopping centers.

DEAR MR. WOLF:
AT CHICK-FIL-A, OUR
HIGH TOP MERINGUE
ON THE LEMON PIE IS
MADE FROM FRESH EGG
WHITES!

JIM COLLINS

52384-C

dp DEXTER PRESS, INC.

PLACE
STAMP
HERE

Post Card

MR. LARRY WOLF
THE ROUSE COMPANY
COLUMBIA, MD.
21043

Postcards to the Rouse Company

After several weeks, I received a telephone call: "Stop the cards; we will make a deal."

If I were easily discouraged, we would not have the location in Perimeter Mall—and a restaurant that has been one of Chick-fil-A's top performing mall locations for forty years. Not only that, but making the deal to locate in Perimeter Mall opened doors with many other developers, and it established for us a mutually beneficial, ongoing relationship with the Rouse Company.

The losses that people experience when they are easily discouraged are immeasurable. On the other hand, the gains from overcoming discouragement may be difficult to measure but are major contributors to our success and satisfaction. I recommend that you work to develop this same attitude.

Do not be easily discouraged.

─────── PRINCIPLE 32 ───────
Be Thankful for Strong-Willed Critics

Most people do not like strong-willed critics who question their actions, hold them accountable, or express opposing views. That is unfortunate, because they are missing out on an opportunity for growth. That's right! Strong-willed criticism is a wonderful opportunity for self-development, and those who avoid it will never know what they missed.

All of my life, I have enjoyed a good fight. (That is, of course, as long as there is no physical pain for anyone or any blood shed—especially mine!) What I enjoy about a fight of ideas, when aggressively slugged out with a passionate and well-rehearsed opponent in one corner and me in the opposite, is that it clarifies my thinking. A worthy opponent can cause me to understand a position, provide an opportunity for me to clarify my own position, and offer a chance to weigh the benefits of different ideas. Only after I test my position in this way am I prepared to preach, practice, and persuade others to accept my position. It is a healthy process that must be faced head-on and never avoided.

Let me give you an example. During my late twenties and early thirties, I taught a Sunday school class for young married couples at my church. We were all about the same age and most of us had young children. There were sharp people in that class and many of them were comfortable enough to speak up or disagree. I was blessed to have one special person in that class—let's call him Joe. He was an airline pilot, and when he entered his cockpit, he was fully prepared to fly. He expected no less of his teacher.

Joe was intelligent, had an almost photographic memory, could debate skillfully, and knew a great deal about the Bible. Along with several others, he made certain I tied up all the loose ends in my lesson presentations. Joe was the one most responsible for holding me accountable, pushing me to grow and develop into a more effective teacher. He motivated me to always be at my best, and I had to invest more time in the preparation for this class because the focus was not only on what to say to the class—the lesson also had to be prepared in a way that was acceptable to Joe. The process inspired me personally and spiritually. Thank God for the many friends like Joe I have had in my life over the years.

At Chick-fil-A, we attracted many independent-minded, entrepreneurial, and high-spirited Operators. I loved them! They were the mustangs mentioned previously—people who lived on the edge of, and sometimes beyond, their authority. Mustangs charge and pull ahead very quickly, and some Operators pulled really hard. That was okay with me! I appreciated this kind the most. The scuffles were productive and we all grew and profited from them. They stimulated my personal and professional growth. I am thankful for the mustangs in my life.

Some people prefer dealing with milder, more submissive personalities who do not tend to make waves. However, few things change if everyone is concerned about maintaining the status quo. Mustangs get ahead faster because mustangs take charge and move things forward.

As a creative follower, be an example—be a mustang! Think for yourself, push the envelope, and live on the edge of your authority. You are much more valuable on the leading edge than you are in a safer, more sedate place where nothing much happens. At the same time, take it a step further: cultivate and encourage mustangs to keep you on your toes.

Be thankful for strong-willed critics.

PRINCIPLE 33

Never Assume
What You Can Verify

One of the most thought-provoking people I have ever known was Dr. Anthony A. Malizia, Jr., an outstanding urologist. Tony was not only my doctor; he was also a friend whose company I enjoyed. Whenever we parted, I was intellectually inspired, in addition to feeling better physically. I particularly remember the day he started our conversation with this bold statement: "The greatest enemy of learning is knowing."

Now, just stop reading and think. Does your life experience confirm that? Mine surely does. Most of us are stuck with the concept of "I know what I know." Oh, my! It makes me feel very foolish when I think of how many times that assumption has gotten me in trouble. How about you?

I have found it necessary to remind myself that, even though I know a little about something, there is always more that I don't know. Also, although I may have been current on a particular subject at some time in the past, what I knew may be obsolete information today.

Even though the incident I am about to describe may not have been the worst day of my life, I have often described it that way. Even if it was not the worst, you will probably agree with me that it was a lousy day. And guess who was at fault? Yes! I am the guilty one.

In 1966, when I was a restaurant design consultant, I was

retained by a partnership formed to purchase an existing hotel in Albany, Georgia, remodel it, and add a first-class restaurant. The partnership offered me the food service design work only if I could complete the initial survey, work out the space requirements with the architect, prepare preliminary plans, and have a budget ready—all in time to meet a nearly impossible deadline. I agreed and took the job. Late in the evening before the nine o'clock meeting in Albany, the material was ready to present.

No problem. I had other clients in Albany and frequently took the Southern Airways morning flight. I knew it left Atlanta at 6:45 a.m. and would allow me to arrive at just the right time for the meeting with the partnership. I called Southern Airways and reserved a seat on the morning flight and called Avis for a rental car.

In those days, you did not have to get to the Atlanta airport much ahead of your departure time. If you had no baggage to check, twenty minutes was plenty of time. When I arrived at the Southern Airways counter, I learned that the departure time had changed to six o'clock and the plane had already left the gate. I knew the flight departure time used to be 6:45, because I flew it often, but I had not learned that the departure time had been changed.

Because the next flight was in the afternoon, I was in trouble. But I am not easily discouraged, so I called my friend Guy Hill, who operated a fixed-base and charter service at the Fulton County Airport. He didn't have a pilot available, but he offered to come himself and fly me to Albany so I could make that nine o'clock meeting. In just a few minutes he arrived in a Cessna 210, a fast single-engine plane with retractable landing gear. As we approached Albany, I realized I had just enough time to rent a car and make the meeting. Guy had flown fast and at a high altitude to get me there on time. He made a very fast spiral descent to land.

That turned out to be a very bad idea! A Cessna 210 is not a pressurized plane. I had a sinus infection and the rapid increase in pressure made its way to my ears. I tried everything to make the pain go away. I alternated between yawning, swallowing, and pinching my nose while forcing air out to build up pressure, yet no relief came. By the time we reached the ground, the piercing pain in both of my ears was almost more than I could bear. Plus, I could barely hear anything. But I was determined to be on time, no matter what.

I rushed to the Avis counter for my car, only to have the rental agent hand back my driver's license and say, "Mr. Collins, your license has expired." But there was a taxi available. Nearly deaf and in pain, I made it to the meeting by nine o'clock.

The meeting was long. That pain in my ears and the difficulty I was having hearing made it seem as if it lasted forever. However, I left satisfied that I had kept my commitment to be on time, to be fully prepared, and to present a plan that would be accepted. I had paid a high price to fulfill that commitment because I had assumed what I could have verified.

This story goes on. I boarded the airliner that departed

Albany that afternoon, but we did not land in Atlanta—we returned to the Albany airport because the landing gear wouldn't retract. The replacement plane sent from Atlanta, an old DC-3 that seemed barely airworthy, didn't arrive until after midnight. Of course, DC-3s did not have pressurized cabins either. There is more, but I will stop here.

As a consultant, I never hesitated to do more than my clients expected, even if the required time or my expenses exceeded my original estimate and I had to absorb the additional cost myself. But when I delivered what I had promised and my client did not feel obligated to pay me, it really disappointed me. Unfortunately, I found myself in that situation in this case, and that is why I do not hesitate in calling this a really lousy day. The client refused to pay me the fee we had agreed upon!

Why did all of this happen to me on that day? Dr. Malizia was right; the greatest enemy of learning is knowing. I thought I knew. I assumed what I could have verified. Just 15 seconds is all the time I needed to confirm the departure time of that flight to Albany. It is no big deal to keep track of the expiration date of my driver's license. I could have verified it, but I didn't. As much as I flew, I knew how to deal with my chronic ear and sinus problem. I could have prevented the pain and temporary deafness. All I had to do was ask Guy to descend slowly, but I didn't.

How many incidents like this will it take for you to adopt Followership Principle 33: Never Assume What You Can Verify? I would be too embarrassed to tell you how many times it took me to learn this. Maybe you learn more quickly than I did.

As difficult as it has been for me to condition myself to never assume what I can verify, it has been easy compared to avoiding the assumptions of others when I need verified information. Of all the followership principles, this may be the one I have repeated most often to others. By repeating this principle many times, I was able to condition others to verify information before they brought it me. They wanted to be prepared to say yes when I asked, "Did you verify this?" In turn, when I informed my boss, I did not intend to leave myself exposed if he asked, "Are you sure?" You cannot be an effective creative follower unless you practice this principle.

Never assume what you can verify.

--------- PRINCIPLE 34 ---------
Use Actions and Symbols

The following is essential to taking Creative Followership to the next level and beyond. The role of the executive includes interpreting and clearly communicating what the leader wants, in a form that everyone in the organization or your area of responsibility can understand, practice, and apply. How will you accomplish this? One way is through the use of actions and symbols.

The creative follower must understand the power of action. It is best to act! People respond better to seeing a person in action than they do to just hearing someone talk. This is a role for both the leader and the creative follower—if you have something you want to communicate, it is best to teach others by using some type of action. This is a key element for the creative follower whose job it is to convey the leader's purpose to everyone in the organization.

One of Truett's concerns with regard to Chick-fil-A restaurants is cleanliness. Many people in the organization remind Operators to keep their restaurants clean and presentable, but sometimes things fall below the acceptable level and a clearer message is necessary.

There are many ways to communicate with action. When I visited restaurants, it was my practice to park my car and, before entering, walk around the parking lot looking for trash. I wanted those working inside the restaurant to look outside and see a guy in a suit picking up trash. When I entered the building, there was always some discussion about my cleaning up the parking lot while wearing a suit and tie. My point was that if the parking lot needs cleaning, it needs cleaning now—by the first available person, regardless of who that may be.

This example demonstrates how easily a creative follower can assist the leader in the communication and teaching process. The journey to personal success through assisting your leader in reaching her goals is not something subservient or insignificant. Responsibility and roles are not something that must be handed down; they are taken as one assumes more and more responsibility in the organization, and this often results from assisting the leader in communicating the unifying purpose through executable actions. As I have mentioned many times, it also includes doing the things the boss does not do well or does not like to do.

Moreover, there is value in developing symbols in the communication process. Picking up trash is an action, but I also used many symbols in my role as a creative follower. One symbol is the paper clip, or gem clip. Around the Chick-fil-A headquarters, this symbol became so strong that some referred to them as "Jimmy clips."

Why gem clips? I chose gem clips because they are seemingly insignificant things that are easy to take for granted. People will leave gem clips by the copy machine, drop them on the floor, or toss them in the trash can. Something that Truett holds in high regard is avoiding waste. Gem clips are not free, and they can be used over and over. There is no need to toss them in the trash still clipped to the papers they are holding together. Therefore, I adopted gem clips as a symbol. I was not obsessed with gem clips; I was concerned with a conscious awareness of needless waste.

This symbol became so attached to me that on my twentieth anniversary at Chick-fil-A, I was presented with a caricature drawing of myself, with everything themed around the symbol of the gem clip. On my desk in the drawing are many books showing titles with the word gem in them, and there are jars and trays of used gem clips on the desk.

Jimmy and wife, Oleta, with caricature picture presented on his 20th anniversary at Chick-fil-A

I didn't mind the ribbing because it indicated that I had succeeded in getting my message across: "Don't throw away gem clips if they can be reused." I knew this would be translated to other items in the office and would help many to understand the problem of needless waste.

Symbols are everywhere, and they are powerful tools that the creative follower should use as he or she grows in influence and responsibility within the organization. Furthermore, as your responsibility increases due to your successful followership, be aware that more and more eyes are watching you. If I had ignored trash in the parking lot or tossed away a gem clip in front of someone, the results could have been disastrous to my reputation! Guard your reputation with regard to things both big and small.

Picking up trash in the parking lot and saving gem clips are just two of many actions and symbols I used. Make your work and your message memorable through the power of actions and symbols. The task of interpreting and delivering the unifying purpose in an executable form is both challenging and rewarding. Find actions and symbols to help make the message and values of your leader or boss stick in the minds of other followers or workers.

Use actions and symbols.

———— **PRINCIPLE 35** ————
Avoid Executive Privilege

As you learn Creative Followership and grow in your relationship with your leader, you will get opportunities that other employees may not have. As your success increases, so will the rewards. However, the benefits do not define you or your unifying purpose with the leader.

Creative followers who are doing their jobs well will see their boss's status in the organization improve. With the advancement of your boss comes advancement for you. As more opportunities open up for the leader, he or she may make these same things available to the follower who has played a key part in the promotion. But be very aware and alert to wonderful "opportunities"—they could be your undoing.

A special assigned parking space, authorization to fly first class, or a key to the executive restroom may make you feel good even while it undermines the spirit of cooperation you previously enjoyed with your coworkers.

During my time as the second-level executive at Chick-fil-A, I was authorized to take advantage of my position, but I chose not to. I maintained the role of employee rather than privileged executive. Truett allowed me a large number of privileges, but I was never comfortable taking advantage of the opportunities and I was determined not to fall into the ego trap. It ruins relationships with the people working with you.

What happens when people become caught up in fully exercising their rewards and privileges? Often, they will offend those who work with them but do not have the benefit of similar privileges. I did not want a barrier to separate me from my coworkers; I depended upon them. I needed to maintain the relationship of approachability with everyone in the organization. As Dwight D. Eisenhower put it, "A people that values its privileges above its principles soon loses both."

I believe there is danger in executive privilege. Certain privileges are easy to understand when they benefit the owner, but they may not look appropriate when they are claimed by someone working *for* the owner. The owner's behavior can easily be explained; he is doing something with his own money. However, it is a different story for a follower.

It is wiser to do without than to claim every benefit and privilege available to you. Do not lose your head! Remember that the perks did not get you where you are. You can live fine without them and you will be more likely to advance in your career by not letting them be a part of your career path. As Lincoln said, "Nearly all men can stand adversity, but if you want to test a man's character, give him power."

A RESTROOM OF MY OWN?

In 1981, Chick-fil-A moved into a new home office building. Truett Cathy is the owner of the building and the company. He can build whatever he chooses. He planned his new office with his own private restroom, which included a shower. Truett often had speaking engagements two or three times per week. Many were in the evening, and he needed a private place to refresh and dress for the evening.

However, when he asked me, the number-two officer, whether I wanted a restroom of my own, it took me about three-quarters of a second to say no. I had no need for a restroom of my own. Besides, if I got a restroom of my own, who else would expect to get one? Would the senior vice presidents expect the same? What about ordinary vice presidents? Would it extend to the senior directors? Where would the line be drawn? I knew the ideal place; I had the line drawn just above me.

WHAT DOES PRIDE LOOK LIKE?

Pride is not just one of the seven deadly sins; it actually is the deadliest one of all, because all the others flow from it in one way or another. Like beauty, pride is in the eye of the beholder. Others see us not as we think we are but as they perceive us to be. That is why we must step outside of ourselves and see our behavior as it comes across to those who are evaluating what we say and do.

Everyone we meet measures our behavior by what we say and do. They want to be sure we "walk the talk." If our walk does not match our talk, they write us off as phonies, fakes, or frauds; we can easily render ourselves unworthy of respect. We all have opportunities to learn about this as children, and by adulthood most of us are well prepared to deal with it.

Pride is an attitude of superiority. It is a way of thinking that we have an edge, whether it is in our physical appearance, our intellectual prowess, or our social and professional skills. It is the opposite of humility. Unfortunately, many assertive people have a negative view of humility. They just don't like the idea of being humble.

There was a time when I thought humility was thinking less of yourself. Many years ago, while listening to a sermon on pride by my friend, the senior minister of Southwest Christian Church, Dr. James W. Dyer, Jr., I wrote in the margin of my Bible a quote: "Humility is not thinking less of yourself; humility is not thinking of yourself." The quote may have been a paraphrase of C. S. Lewis, or it may simply have been my observation about the life of one of the humblest and greatest men I have ever known, Jim Dyer. Jim understood humility. He lived it. Does that statement sound easy to live out in the real world? Try it and you will see!

Let me give you an example of how I learned why I should not think of myself. During my son Ken's high school years, we moved him to a new school. I met one of his coaches, a man I really liked. Our friendship was growing steadily. One day this coach asked me what I did for a living. I replied, "I'm the vice president of Chick-fil-A." But I didn't get the reaction I was anticipating.

Do you know those roll-down doors made of steel slats used in hallways to divide buildings in case of a fire? As soon as I told him my title at Chick-fil-A, it was like one of those doors came crashing down between us. It was the last conversation we ever had.

Afterward, I thought a lot about that incident. Was I prideful in the way I spoke? Maybe. Was he overly sensitive? Possibly. All that matters is that I did not measure up to his expectations. I recognized that I couldn't control his response, but I certainly could change the way I presented myself. If humility is not thinking of myself, it also involves getting others not to think of me.

A new course of action had to be implemented. After that incident, when I met new people I almost never told them my title. They might find out later, but I didn't tell them immediately; even now I do not tell people what my title was before I retired. As a creative follower, you may need to consider a similar plan. There are ways to get around the question and still give a respectful answer.

When asked, "What do you do?" here are the two replies

that I used. Notice that both redirect the person's thoughts away from me. When asked, I initially answered, "I work for Chick-fil-A," and the next question almost always was "Which one?" That's because people think of the food and the restaurant where it is served, not the corporate headquarters. I directed their thinking to food and the restaurants, not to me. My answer to this follow-up question, when I confessed I worked at the home office, usually brought out a sigh of disappointment and a simple "Oh."

The implication for customers is that the restaurant is where the real action is; what goes on at the corporate office is less important than where they get their food. Of course, they are right. At that point I would shift gears and ask about their experience as customers.

Some people would persist and would come back with "So, what do you do at the home office?" One reply I liked to use was, "I am responsible for encouragement." I would continue, "Everyone needs encouragement, and anyone can be an encourager." From there I would draw the questioner into a conversation about encouragement.

There also were times when I was talking with people who knew what I did but wanted more information. I would shift their attention with my other reply: "I do what Truett Cathy does not like to do." From there I would draw them into a conversation about doing what the boss does not like to do.

Almost no one ever came back to ask me again about

what I did or about my job title. If I didn't think it was a big deal, they wouldn't think it was either. Since retiring, I still use a slightly modified version of the same two replies. I have found that, once people accept you for who you are, what you do is not a big issue.

Remember, your job as a creative follower is to make the boss look good, not to draw attention to yourself. Exercise caution if you work for a leader with a public profile. Your goal is not to make headlines. It is not about you; it is about the leader and the purpose.

Avoid executive privilege.

CONCLUSION

The end of this book is not the end of the story most important to you—your story! Now is a good time to sit down and write the story of your life. Start with the end in mind. How does your story end? Describe that story in detail. Start with who you want to be, then where you want to be and what you want to be doing. Next, decide what you need to do to translate that ending into a reality. Then get started at once.

Start where you are, and never hesitate to keep moving to where you want to be at the end of your story.

The end of this book is the beginning of your opportunity to see the benefits of Creative Followership, which last a lifetime. Not only do they last but also they get better and better as you put them into practice. As you assimilate more of the principles of Creative Followership into your life, you will also find many opportunities to create followership principles of your own. Creative Followership is an adventure of discovery, not a mindless adherence to a list of rules. Be bold, take risks, invent, modify, but most of all, have fun. Live life to its fullest.

The choices you make now will determine your future. Take that first step: choose your boss! Choose someone worthy of your confidence, trust, and loyalty; find a leader with a unifying purpose you can enthusiastically support. To enjoy the maximum benefits of the practice of Creative Followership, I recommend you choose a leader with a great shadow.

When I retired, my coworkers made a video to be shown to the Chick-fil-A Operators at the last annual Operators Seminar I would attend. My wife, Oleta, was one of those interviewed, and she described what happened when I returned home after meeting with Truett the day I accepted his job offer. She recalled, "He said he was going to work for Truett Cathy; he didn't say he was going to work for Chick-fil-A." Oleta's memory was perfect. I had chosen a boss (who was a leader), not a position or a corporation.

As a follower of Truett Cathy, I have been in the shadow of greatness. In that shadow, I discovered satisfaction, success, and opportunities to practice my principles of Creative Followership. I can wholeheartedly recommend these principles to you because they have been tested and found worthy.

But there is more to my story. I also practice another followership, one that helps me in my daily practice of Creative Followership. I am a follower of the greatest of all leaders. The Leader of leaders, the Boss of bosses, the King of kings . . . Jesus. My benefits from this followership will go beyond this lifetime and into eternity because I will live forever . . . in the shadow of greatness.